CONCILIUM

THEOLOGY IN THE AGE OF RENEWAL

CONCILIUM

CONCILIUM / VOL. 12

LITURGY

THE
CHURCH
WORSHIPS

Volume 12

CONCILIUM
theology in the age of renewal

PAULIST PRESS
NEW YORK, N.Y. / GLEN ROCK, N.J.

NIHIL OBSTAT: Joseph F. Donahue, S.J., S.T.D.
Censor Deputatus

IMPRIMATUR: ✠ Bernard J. Flanagan, D.D.
Bishop of Worcester

January 27, 1966

The Nihil Obstat and Imprimatur are official declarations that a book or pamphlet is free of doctrinal or moral error. No implication is contained therein that those who have granted the Nihil Obstat and Imprimatur agree with the contents, opinions or statements expressed.

Library of Congress Catalogue Card Number: 66-17730

Suggested Decimal Classification: 264.02

BOOK DESIGN: Claude Ponsot

Paulist Press assumes responsibility for the accuracy of the English translations in this Volume.

PAULIST PRESS
EXECUTIVE OFFICES: 304 W. 58th Street, New York, N.Y. and 21 Harristown Road, Glen Rock, N.J.
Executive Publisher: John A. Carr, C.S.P.
Executive Manager: Alvin A. Illig, C.S.P.
Asst. Executive Manager: Thomas E. Comber, C.S.P.

EDITORIAL OFFICES: 304 W. 58th Street, New York, N.Y.
Editor: Kevin A. Lynch, C.S.P.
Managing Editor: Urban P. Intondi

Printed and bound in the United States of America by
The Colonial Press Inc., Clinton, Mass.

CONTENTS

PART II

BIBLIOGRAPHICAL SURVEY

PART III

DOCUMENTATION CONCILIUM

PART I
ARTICLES

Joseph Lécuyer, C.S.Sp./*Rome, Italy*

The Liturgical Assembly: Biblical and Patristic Foundations

S ince the Constitution on the Sacred Liturgy has drawn our attention to the traditional importance of the liturgical assembly in the life of the Church, it is worthwhile to show that the teaching of Vatican Council II is in perfect accord with the Church's most authentic tradition and rooted in the New Testament itself. Therefore, we shall first study the New Testament material and then summarize, in our second part, the conclusions that the most ancient Christian tradition drew from it.

I

THE NEW TESTAMENT MATERIAL

After the Lord's ascension, the apostles gathered in "the upper room where they were staying" (Acts 1, 13). Some regard this as the same room in which Jesus celebrated the Last Supper and appeared on Easter night (Luke 24, 33), perhaps also the room in which the disciples were assembled on Pentecost (Acts 2, 1); O. Cullmann thinks it can be located in the house of John's (surnamed Mark) mother (Acts 12, 12).[1] At any rate, St. Luke

[1] O. Cullmann, *La foi et le culte dans l'Eglise primitive* (Neuchâtel-Paris, 1963), p. 107.

3

continues: "All these *with one mind* continued steadfastly in prayer with the women and Mary, the mother of Jesus, and with his brethren." The statement that all were praying "with one mind" (*homothymadon*) is noteworthy. L. Cerfaux points out that this is a characteristic word in the first part of Acts and, with the exception of Romans 15, 6 (also in a context of liturgical prayer), is found only in that book.[2]

In this atmosphere of common ("unanimous") prayer, the disciples obeyed their master's instruction to remain in Jerusalem and "wait for the promise of the Father" (Acts 1, 4). This, then, is the spiritual context in which the event of Pentecost, which fulfills that expectation, must be understood: the Spirit descends on the community which is persevering in prayer "with one mind", while they are "all together in one place" (Acts 2, 1). The translation "in one place" is certainly far from exhausting the meaning of the Greek, *epi to auto,* already used in Acts 1, 15 and again in 2, 44 and 2, 47. In the first part of Acts this expression "has a pregnant, technical meaning, expressing union in the Christian society, the community",[3] a real union of minds and hearts. The Pentecost narrative in Acts becomes more comprehensible if we recall that in New Testament times the Jewish Pentecost had become the feast of the giving of the Law on Sinai.[4] The Jewish accounts of the gathering at Sinai also insist on the unanimity, the union of hearts, that governed the assembly gathered about the holy mountain, where all had but one mind as they waited for and received the Law.[5] Further, the Septuagint

[2] L. Cerfaux, "La première communauté chrétienne à Jerusalem," in *Recueil Lucien Cerfaux* II (1954), p. 129.

[3] *Ibid.,* p. 152. Some manuscripts of Acts, it may be noted, also repeat *homothymadon* in 2, 1 as well as in 1, 14, and later in 2, 46; 5, 12; 15, 25. Cf. J. Dupont, "La première Pentecôte chrétienne," *Assemblées du Seigneur* 51 (Bruges, 1961), p. 42: "They are together, not only by reason of the place they are in, but also by the union of their hearts."

[4] Cf. G. Kretschmar, "Himmelfahrt und Pfingsten," in *Zeitschrift für Kirchengeschichte* 66 (1954-55), pp. 209-53; B. Noack, "The Day of Pentecost in Jubilees, Qumran and Acts," in *Annual of the Swedish Theological Institute* 1 (1962), pp. 73-95; especially R. Le Déaut, "Pentecôte et tradition juive," in *Spiritus* 7 (1961), pp, 127-44, reproduced in *Assemblées du Seigneur* 51 (1961), pp. 22-38.

[5] See Ex. 19, 8 and the targumic and rabbinic commentaries on the

describes this as "the day of the assembly", literally the day of the *ecclesia* (Deut. 4, 10; 9, 10; 18, 16), a phrase repeated in Stephen's discourse in Acts 7, 38. But this same word *ecclesia* is also used for the primitive community, which therefore is to be understood, particularly on the day of Pentecost, as the eschatological continuation of the desert community; it is the assembly summoned by God to the new Sinai, which is the mountain of Sion,[6] there to receive the new law and enter into the new covenant.

To these men united in prayer and expectation God intends to manifest himself as he did on Sinai, making his presence sensible to their eyes and ears,[7] or rather making sensible the dynamic presence of the glorified Christ, now the dispenser of the Spirit (cf. Acts 2, 33). Thus, filled with the Holy Spirit they all begin to speak "in foreign tongues, even as the Holy Spirit prompted them to speak" (Acts 2, 4), and the purpose of this sudden explosion of speech is to "proclaim the wonderful works of God" (Acts 2, 11).[8] The coming of the Spirit thus inaugurates in the community the movement of thanksgiving, of "eucharist", which is the foundation of the Christian cult and which unites peoples of all tongues in one proclamation and one act of praise, announcing the wonders wrought by God in Jesus whom he has raised from the dead (Acts 2, 24. 31f.), exalted to his right hand (Acts 2, 33f.), made Lord and Christ (Acts 2, 36). From the hour of this first assembly the proclamation of the Lordship of the risen Christ takes the first place, and it is the Spirit of God who supplies the inspiration.

Luke's narrative goes on to state that the Christians "continued steadfastly in the teaching of the apostles and in the communion of the breaking of bread and in the prayers" (Acts

biblical accounts of the Sinai theophany; the principal texts are mentioned in J. Lécuyer, *Le sacrifice de la nouvelle alliance* (Le Puy-Paris, 1962), pp. 38, 156.

[6] See *ibid.* pp. 25, 33-35, 50f., 62f., 70, for this typological equivalence between Sinai and Sion.

[7] For the connections with the Sinai assembly, see *ibid.* pp. 156f.

[8] Although the word is used only once in the New Testament, the Greek translation of the Old Testament usually employs it for the wonders wrought by God during the liberation from Egypt and the Exodus.

2, 42). "And continuing daily with one accord (*homothymadon*) in the temple, and breaking bread in their houses,[9] they took their food with gladness and simplicity of heart, praising God . . ." (Acts 2, 46f). Here we see the beginning of the custom of daily reunion in private homes[10] where, in an atmosphere of joy, of divine praise and of prayer, the eucharist was celebrated[11] during a fraternal meal. This description of the first Jerusalem community and the parallel "summaries" in the following chapters (Acts 4, 32; 5, 12f.)[12] emphasize the unity and unanimity that ruled in the community. For our present purpose we must especially notice the clear intent to portray the daily gathering as the privileged place and sign of that profound unity (cf. 2, 46 and 47). The repetition of the expression *epi to auto* (Acts 2, 44.47) is full of meaning, especially in verse 47 where it is evidently understood as equivalent to "in the Church"; as a matter of fact several manuscripts and versions actually take it in that sense.[13] The community assembly actualizes the Church and in some way is identified with it.

After their imprisonment, Peter and John return to the assembly (Acts 4, 20); all raise their voices together (*homothymadon*) in prayer and once more, in this assembly united in a unanimous prayer, the Holy Spirit displays his gifts (Acts 4, 31f.).

[9] Perhaps it would be better to translate "at home" here as in Acts 5, 42, as Cullmann suggests, indicating thereby the house in which these gatherings regularly took place, possibly the same one in which the Pentecost theophany occurred. It is a private home as opposed to the temple, by a custom attested elsewhere: 1 Cor. 16, 19; Rom. 16, 5; Philem. 2; Col. 4, 15. Cf. O. Cullmann, *La foi et le culte dans l'Eglise primitive* (Neuchâtel-Paris, 1963), p. 107.

[10] For a fairly long time in some places there was no special place built for worship. For Roman practice, see R. Vieillard, *Recherches sur les origines de la Rome chrétienne* (Rome, ²1959). A house furnished as a church about 232 A.D. was discovered at Dura-Europus in 1930.

[11] This is the meaning that the great majority of exegetes and historians of the Church finds today in the "breaking of bread".

[12] See especially P. Benoit, "Remarques sur les sommaires des Actes II, IV et V," in *Exégèse et théologie* II, pp. 181ff.

[13] See the recent study of M. Wilcox, *The Semitisms of Acts* (Oxford, 1965), pp. 93-100. The expression seems, at least indirectly, derived from a formula that occurs at Qumran, and which actually meant "the community",

The Acts of the Apostles mention other assemblies also: at Jerusalem (Acts 6, 2-6; 12, 12), at Antioch (14, 27; 15, 30), especially at Troas where the Christians, united for "the breaking of bread" on Sunday the first day of the week, hear a long discourse from Paul (Acts 20, 7f.).

The Assembly in Paul's Writings

Many passages in Paul's writings refer to liturgical assemblies in the homes of individuals (1 Cor. 16, 19; Rom. 16, 5; Philem. 2; Col. 4, 15): the word used is *ecclesia.*[14] The most important passages are in the first Epistle to the Corinthians.

At Corinth the eucharist was celebrated as a common meal (1 Cor. 11, 20). But instead of actually putting everything in common for a fraternal meal, groups had formed, connected by blood or friendship, who were eating their provisions with no concern for the others, without waiting until all had arrived, without care for those who were poor. Accordingly, some had an abundant feast while others could not even satisfy their hunger.

Such gatherings not governed by a spirit of charity, declares Paul, do more harm than good (1 Cor. 11, 17), for "the Church of God" is mocked in them (v. 22): this is no longer the "Lord's Supper" (v. 20). To act in this manner is to eat the bread or drink the cup of the Lord *unworthily.* Whoever offends in that way "will be guilty of the body and blood of the Lord", that is, he makes himself responsible for the death of Christ by joining those who crucified him,[15] for he does not distinguish the Lord's body (vv. 27-29).

The full force of Paul's reasoning becomes apparent when we recall that he has previously established the unity of Christ's body, which is the Church, on the foundation of the unity of the bread in which all Christians communicate (1 Cor. 10, 16f.). The body of Christ is at the same time the body in which we communicate and the body of the Church of which we are a part. To divide the latter by breaking the unity of the assembly

[14] Cf. O. Cullmann, *La foi et le culte dans l'Eglise primitive* (Neuchâtel-Paris, 1948), p. 107.

[15] Cf. J. Leenhardt, *Le sacrement de la sainte Cène* (Neuchâtel-Paris, 1948), p. 87.

is to destroy the body of Christ, while at the same time claiming to be united to it by communion. Thus, Paul's thought is clear: the assembly is not merely any gathering; it is the Church itself, the body of Christ, and every offense against the assembly is an offense against the Lord's body.

The assembly is so important in Paul's eyes that even the use of the charisms of the Holy Spirit is to be regulated in accordance with the demands of the assembly's welfare. Those he declares preferable are the charisms which "edify" the assembly (1 Cor. 14, 3); the others, even though they are useful to those who possess them (v. 4) or can make an impression on unbelievers (v. 22), if they are not profitable for the entire assembly, if the other members cannot join them by their *Amen* (v. 16), must yield: the norm of their usefulness is "that all may learn and all may be encouraged" (v. 31), and for that it is indispensable that "all things be done properly and in order" (v. 40).

Paul is not unaware of the value of these spiritual gifts. They are all gifts of the Spirit, manifestations of his presence in the Church and particularly in the assembly; the very cult in which the Lordship of Christ is proclaimed can be performed only under the action of the Holy Spirit (1 Cor. 12, 3). This manifestation of the Spirit can take varied forms but "the manifestation of the Spirit is given to everyone for common profit" (v. 7): this common usefulness, then, will be the guiding rule in determining the greater or lesser place to be accorded the initiative of different members of the assembly. For this requirement of charity and unity every member of the assembly should be prepared to sacrifice his own preferences, even when he believes an interior movement of the Spirit is involved: "For God is a God of peace, not of disorder" (1 Cor. 14, 33).

The local assembly will also have to take into consideration other Churches and their customs, that is, the universal Church, present certainly in the local assembly but extending beyond it. Because of this principle, Paul imposes on women the wearing of veils in the assembly (1 Cor. 11, 16) and forbids them to speak there (1 Cor. 14, 33f.). They must not act without considering the whole: "What, was it from you that the Word of God went forth? Or was it unto you only that it reached?" (1 Cor. 14, 36). Here we can glimpse the stage attained by a visible and responsible authority in the conduct of the assembly in which a minimum of regulation is necessary.[16]

The Epistle to the Hebrews

The Epistle to the Hebrews refers several times to the Christian assembly, and these references are inspired by a comparison with the assembly of the people of the old covenant during their stay in the desert[17] and with the liturgical assemblies in the temple.[18]

It seems that the recipients of the epistle had shown a certain negligence in attending the assemblies; they had become "careless for instructions" (5, 11) and some had the habit of forsaking the assembly (10, 25). For that negligence the author displays severity: Christians, even more than the Hebrew people in the desert, should be attentive to the teachings they receive "for fear of being led astray" (2, 1); they should guard their fidelity, exhort and encourage one another day after day (3, 13). The Good News that the faithless Jews heard is no good to them "because they did not remain in communion by faith with those who heard" (4, 2): communion in faith with other believers is a condition of salvation.

The *confession,* or profession of faith, required of the Christian (4, 14; 10, 23) must be understood then as a public profession before the community, the object of which is Jesus himself, "apostle and high priest" (3, 1). If he has entered the true sanctuary of heaven, Christians, too, can be sure of being able to gain entrance (10, 19-21); let them approach then, keeping strong their confession of hope, helping and encouraging one another in charity and good works, and attending their assembly (10, 22-

[16] See the remarks of O. Cullmann, *op. cit. supra,* footnote 14, pp. 125f.

[17] On this point see the brief survey of C. Spicq. *L'Epître aux Hébreux* (individual volume of the *Bible de Jerusalem*), pp. 25-28.

[18] According to F. Schierse, *Verheissung und Heilsvollendung* (Munich, 1955), the Christian liturgical gatherings are a central theme in the Epistle to the Hebrews.

25). This whole passage, full of cultual expressions (especially those we translate by "approach"),[19] reveals that participation in the life of the community, especially in its assemblies, is a strict duty of Christians, whose conscience has been purified that they may "serve the living God" (9, 14); to fail in this is to be separated from the unique sacrifice that wipes out sins (10, 26), to trample on the Son of God, to profane the blood of the covenant in which they have been sanctified, and to outrage the Spirit of grace (10, 29).

Chapter 12 gives a wonderful description of the assembly into which Christians have been introduced by baptism (Heb. 12, 22-24).[20] The description is inspired by the accounts of the assembly or *ecclesia* of Sinai,[21] but the new assembly is identified with the Church itself, the new mount of Sion and heavenly Jerusalem (cf. Gal. 4, 22-26; Apoc. 14, 1); the worship offered there, in a "holy day gathering", unites Christians on earth with the angels, with the spirits of the just who have already attained fulfillment, with Christ himself, mediator of the new covenant, and with his blood. Christ is present in the assembly and his voice is to be heard there speaking from heaven (Heb. 12, 25). When they enter the assembly, then, Christians are mysteriously led into heaven itself; and thus, already receiving "a kingdom that cannot be shaken", they can by grace "offer pleasing service to God with fear and reverence" (Heb. 12, 28).

Before concluding this brief examination of the New Testament, we must also notice a passage of the Epistle of James (2, 2-4): there must be no distinctions in the assembly because of wealth or social condition; such distinctions count for nothing before God, and the assembly's purpose is to reduce what is otherwise divided to the unity of a single body.

[19] The reference to the cult in the verbs *eiserkomai* and *proserkomai* in the epistle has long been recognized: cf. C. Spicq, *L'Epître aux Hébreux* I (Paris, 1952), pp. 281f.

[20] The verb *proselēlythate* is in the perfect, which indicates an act performed at some past time but whose effects remain operative.

[21] Cf. J. Lécuyer, "Ecclesia primitivorum," in *Studiorum Paulinorum Congressus Internationalis Catholicus 1962* II (Rome, 1963), pp. 161-8. Dom Dix has drawn attention to the description of a liturgical assembly

We have to start from these teachings, reflecting on a practice that goes back to the origins of the Church, to penetrate the meaning of the assembly. We will attempt, in the second part of this study, to synthesize the principal doctrinal points by studying the earliest witnesses of the patristic tradition.

II

THE ASSEMBLY ACCORDING TO THE FATHERS

The documents from the beginnings of extra-canonical Christian literature that tell us of the liturgical assembly are so numerous that we can only mention the most important. The best course seems to be to group them under some of the more important themes and so sketch the beginning of a doctrinal synthesis.

1. *The Assembly Is Characteristic of Christian Life*

From the apostolic era, and in conformity with the instructions of the New Testament, the *Didachē* teaches that Christians are to assemble for "the breaking of bread and for thanksgiving".[22] Ignatius of Antioch often stresses this obligation in texts in which the formula of the Acts of the Apostles, *epi to auto,* has the ring of a technical expression. Not to attend the gathering, he tells the Ephesians (5, 2f.), is an act of pride which God will punish; therefore, let them gather more frequently to offer acts of thanksgiving and praise to God (13, 1). He advises the Philadelphians to assemble "with undivided heart" (6, 2); as for the Magnesians (7, 1f.), let them not attempt to justify anything they do outside the common assembly.

These gatherings for worship seemed sufficiently characteristic of the life of Christians that Pliny the Younger thought he should inform Trajan of them: "They follow the practice of gathering on a particular day before dawn, and of addressing a prayer to

---

in Hebrews 12, 23: *The Shape of the Liturgy* (Westminster, 1964), pp. 336f.

[22] *Didachē* 14, 1. Cf. H. Chirat, *L'assemblée chrétienne à l'âge apostolique* (Paris, 1949).

Christ as God." [23] Justin, writing to the Emperor Antoninus, gives a much more detailed description of these assemblies: the assembly includes "all who dwell in the cities or the country-side".[24] With the same intention of making known and explaining the Christians' practices, Tertullian in 197 describes these periodic gatherings in his *Apologeticum*.[25]

As J. Jungmann, following Dom Gregory Dix, remarks,[26] the first Christians seem to have considered the assembly extremely important; they remained faithful to it despite the calumnies that pagans circulated about these gatherings, despite persecutions and all kinds of pressure. During Diocletian's persecution the martyrs of Abitina told their judges: "We cannot forego the assembly of the Lord's Day (*dominica*). The Lord's assembly cannot be interrupted." [27]

2. *Sunday, the Day of the Assembly*

The word *dominicum* used by the Abitina martyrs brings us to a new point. If the Christians came together every day in the beginning (Acts 2, 46; 5, 42), they soon chose one particular day, the one that followed the sabbath (1 Cor. 16, 2; Acts 20, 7), which they called "the Lord's Day" (Apoc. 1, 10); this is the day on which the *Didachē* commands the gathering for the breaking of the bread and for thanksgiving.[28] Ignatius of Antioch gives the reasons for the choice: this day, the one after the sabbath (Matt. 28, 1), is that on which Christ was raised from the dead.[29] The very choice of the word *kyriakē* (*dominica*) suggests a connection with the resurrection, for that is actually the day, accord-

[23] Pliny the Younger, *Epist. Lib.* x, n. 96.

[24] Justin, *First Apology* 67, 3.

[25] Tertullian, *Apologeticum* 39, 2 (*Corpus christianorum* I, 50); the words used are *coetus, congregatio,* and elsewhere *convocatio, convivium dominicum: Ad Uxorem* II, 4, 2 (*Corp. Christ.* I, 388 and 389).

[26] J. Jungmann, *La liturgie des premiers siècles* (Paris, 1962), pp. 26f.

[27] Ed. T. Ruinart, *Acta primorum martyrum sincera* (Paris, 1689), p. 414. Cf. A. Martimort, "Dimanche, assemblée et paroisse," in *La Maison-Dieu* 57 (1959), p. 70.

[28] *Didachē*, 14, 1. There are two possible readings: *kata kuriakēn de kuriou* (Funk-Bihlmeyer), or *kath' hēmeran de kuriou* (J. Audet), but the meaning is the same.

[29] *Magnes.* IX, 1.

ing to Peter's affirmation, on which the risen Christ became *Kyrios*, Lord and Head of his Church (Acts 2, 36).[30] From the 4th century onward the Greeks called Sunday "Resurrection Day", and the Russians still use the word *Voskresseniye* (resurrection).[31] It was already Tertullian's expression.[32]

Further symbolism is added to the Sunday celebration. Justin, speaking to pagans, designates the day by the name familiar to them, "the Sun's day": so the Christian assembly celebrates, together with Christ's resurrection, the first day of creation on which God created light.[33] It was easy to embellish this theme and celebrate the true Sun of Justice, which Christ is.[34] Further, though Sunday is the first day of the Jewish week, it can also be considered as the *eighth day*, the day following the sabbath; from the time of pseudo-Barnabas and Justin this name will be associated with the theme of the resurrection[35] and later become the subject of some very complicated speculations and reflections.[36]

But the fundamental theme remains that of Christ's resurrection; that is what the assembly always celebrates, as it was already doing on the day of the first Pentecost.

3. *A Festal Assembly*

If the resurrection explains the choice of Sunday, it also accounts for the assembly's atmosphere of joy: a joy expressed in transports of praise on the day of Pentecost, the "overflowing" joy of the first Jerusalem community (Acts 2, 46),[37] the festal atmosphere which the Epistle to the Hebrews describes (Heb. 12, 22) and which can easily be discerned, behind unfortunate ex-

---

[30] J. Jungmann, *op. cit. supra*, footnote 26, p. 39.

[31] *Ibid.*, p. 41.

[32] Tertullian, *De Oratione* 23, 2 (*Corp. Christ.* I, 27).

[33] Justin, *First Apology* 76, 3.

[34] Cf. J. Daniélou, *Bible et liturgie* (Paris, 1951), pp. 344-6, for the principal texts. A trace of the ancient celebration of the sun's day remains in the names Sonntag and Sunday.

[35] Pseudo-Barnabas, *Epist.* XV, 8f.; Justin, *Dialogue* 24, 1.

[36] Cf. J. Danielou, *op. cit.*, pp. 346ff.; J. Jungmann, *op. cit.*, pp. 41f.

[37] See the remarks of R. Bultmann, *Theologisches Wörterbuch zum Neuen Testament*, p. 19.

cesses, in the gatherings at Corinth (1 Cor. 11, 20-22). When Ignatius of Antioch instructs the Philadelphians to send a deacon to Antioch (10, 1), it is "to rejoice with those who are assembled and to glorify the name"; and he advises the Magnesians (7, 1) to gather "in irreproachable joy".

For when the assembled community celebrates the Lord's resurrection it is celebrating its own victory over death.[38] With Christ, as in the Epistle to the Hebrews, the Church has access to the true sanctuary, is already united with the eternal festival of heaven and shares its joy (Heb. 12, 22f.); the celebration of the resurrection anticipates the Lord's victorious return and even now communicates its firstfruits. From the beginning this is expressed in the cry which may be the Church's oldest prayer: "*Maranatha!* Come, Lord Jesus!" (Apoc. 22, 20; 1 Cor. 16, 22; *Didachē* 10, 6).[39] It is also expressed in all the eucharistic liturgies in which the people affirm their certainty that their voice is mingled with those of the angels and saints in heaven,[40] and many other rites manifest the same conviction.[41]

As a matter of fact every assembly, and not only Sunday's, is a feast, a common manifestation of the Church's joy. One of the particular purposes and effects of the assembly is to aid each of its members to support in himself the faith and hope which are the source of a Christian's joy; each brings to it his contribution by

[38] *Constitution on the Sacred Liturgy*, Art. 2. The Constitution often returns to this subject: cf. Arts. 5f, 10, 47, 61, 81, 102, 104, 106f, 109f. Notice the use of the word "celebration", which itself implies a festal atmosphere. It is well known too that in antiquity the command to pray standing on Sunday and the prohibition against bending the knee on that day (and during the paschal season as well) are due to the fact that Sunday is the day of the resurrection: "He who is raised must remain standing to pray, for he who raises him remains standing; thus, whoever has died and risen with Christ remains standing" (*Const. Apost.*, VII, 45, 1). For paschaltide considered as a great Sunday, see R. Cabie's recent book *La Pentecôte* (Tournai, 1965), pp. 46-60.

[39] Cf. O. Cullmann, *op. cit.*, p. 111.

[40] See A. Martimort, "L'assemblée liturgique, mystère liturgique," in *La Maison-Dieu* 40 (1954), pp. 14-6.

[41] Consequently R. Paquier is correct in stating that in her worship the Church "really joins in the affairs of heaven and becomes a participant of Christ and of his kingdom": *Traité de liturgique* (Neuchâtel-Paris, 1954), p. 27.

his own profession of faith (cf. Heb. 10, 23-25), his fraternal presence, and the witness of his unshakable confidence.[42]

4. *Presence of Christ in the Assembly*

If the assembly is a feast, it is not only because of the memory of the resurrection or the faith in Christ's glorious return, but also because of his presence in the midst of his own. Vatican Council II's Constitution on the Liturgy has proclaimed that presence, not only in the minister who offers the eucharist or under the appearances of bread and wine or in the Word proclaimed in the assembly, but also in the assembly itself which prays and gives thanks.[43]

God became present to the assembly at Sinai through the terrifying signs of the theophany; in the new covenant he makes himself visible in his incarnate Son, and the latter continues to be present in his Church through his Spirit. This presence of Christ is not a less "real presence" than that which takes place through transubstantiation: we have to give its full importance to this spiritual presence of Christ in the assembly.

The Fathers of the Church eagerly laid claim to the text of Matthew 18, 20: "Where two or three are gathered together for my sake, there am I in the midst of them," [44] a text found, furthermore, as R. Paquier points out, in an ecclesiological context.[45] Other texts can be cited in which Christ promises to remain with the community of the disciples until the end of time (Matt. 28, 20; cf. John 14, 18; 19, 16, etc.). But it must be emphasized that Christ is present by his Spirit in a special way in his Church whenever it is gathered, whenever it confesses that he is the Lord (1 Cor. 12, 3), and that the charisms distributed to each one work for the profit of all (1 Cor. 12, 4-11): for then his presence is revealed as incarnated in his body, which is the Church (1 Cor. 12, 12f.). That is why the assembly cannot bear

[42] Cf. Jerome, *Comm. in Ep. ad Galatas* 1. 2, c. 4 (*P.L.* 26, col. 378).
[43] *Constitution on the Sacred Liturgy*, Art. 7.
[44] Cf. Chrysostom, *In Annam*, serm. 5, 1 (*P.G.* 54, col. 669); *In Genesim*, serm. 6, 1, etc.
[45] R. Paquier, *op. cit.*, p. 24; see the whole pericope: Matt. 18, 15-20.

divisions within it, for that would be to divide the body of Christ
(1 Cor. 11, 29f.). Thus the assembly appears as a visible sign
of the presence of the Lord, who by his Spirit at every instant
brings about the unity of all the members of his body: the Church
appears in the assembly as the "sacrament of unity".[46]

We reach the same conclusion if, with the Fathers of the
Church, we realize that the assembly itself is the place of the
new cult, the sanctuary in which God dwells. Following the New
Testament (1 Cor. 3, 16; 2 Cor. 6, 16; 1 Pet. 2, 5-9), the
Fathers affirm that the material edifice in which the gathering
takes place is without importance: God "does not dwell in tem-
ples made by hands" (Acts 17, 24). The true sanctuary in which
God dwells is the Church itself, the assembly of earth mysteriously united with the assembly of heaven and really one with
it.[47] We are reminded of Ignatius of Antioch's counsels to the
Magnesians: "All hasten together as into one temple of God, as
about a single altar, in the one Jesus Christ. . . ." [48]

But the Church is the temple of the new cult only to the extent
that it is the body of Christ, the new temple (John 2, 21), the
new tabernacle (John 1, 14) in which God dwells. The ultimate
reason for the presence of Christ in the assembly, then, is that it
is the body of the Lord animated by his Spirit: in the assembly
the Church realizes and fully manifests itself, in the visible presence of the faithful and the invisible presence of the Spirit of
Christ. The Syriac *Didascalia* expresses this very powerfully:

> "Teach the people by precepts and exhortations to at-
> tend the assembly without fail: let them be always present,
> let them never diminish the Church by their absence, and
> let them never deprive the body of Christ of one of its mem-
> bers. Each should take as for himself, not for others, the
> words of Christ: 'He who does not gather with me scatters'
> (Matt. 12, 30; Luke 11, 23). Since you are the members of

---

[46] "Liturgical actions are not private functions, but celebrations of the
Church, which is the 'sacrament of unity', the holy people united and
ordered under the bishops" (*Constitution on the Sacred Liturgy*, Art. 26).

[47] Cf. J. Lécuyer, *op. cit. supra*, footnote 5, pp. 214-9.

[48] Ignatius of Antioch, *Epist. ad Magnes.* 7, 1f.

Christ, you must not be scattered outside the Church by neglecting to come together. In short, since Christ our Head fulfills his promise by becoming present and entering into communion with you, do not you despise yourselves and deprive not the Savior of his members; rend not his body nor scatter it." [49]

5. *The Mystery of the Assembly*

Since Christ is present in the assembly and acts in it through his Spirit, the liturgical assembly is not only a manifestation or expression of the Church, as any gathering of members is an expression of the society to which they belong; the assembly is that, surely,[50] but it is also much more.

When certain New Testament texts identify the assembly and the Church (Acts 2, 47; 1 Cor. 11, 22),[51] that does not mean that the Church exists only when it is gathered in an assembly. But it could be said that the Church exists only inasmuch as its members have been called to the assembly and remain ordered to it. In this respect we may recall that the word *ecclesia* is the translation of the Hebrew *qahal,* which really means an assembly called together by God, particularly the assembly of Sinai. We have seen, too, that several of the New Testament texts described the Christian assembly by reference to that event. According to G. Dix the word *ecclesia* during the first three centuries never means anything but the liturgical assembly or, by extension, those who have a right to participate in it.[52]

On this point the liturgical texts speak eloquently: the passages are countless in which *ecclesia* refers to the assembly actually gathered in prayer.[53] The Church is present wherever, in answer to God's call, she assembles for divine worship; she bap-

---

[49] *Didascalia* II, 59, 1-3 (ed. Funk, p. 170); cf. *Const. Apost.* II, 59, 1-3 (*ibid.* p. 171); Chrysostom, *In 2 Cor.,* hom. 18, 3.

[50] *Constitution on the Sacred Liturgy,* Arts. 2, 41 and 42.

[51] See what we said about this above.

[52] G. Dix, *op. cit. supra,* footnote 22, pp. 19f.

[53] The liturgy frequently uses the expressions *populus tuus, plebs tua, familia tua,* etc.; cf. G. Diekmann, "The Place of Liturgical Worship," in CONCILIUM, Vol. 2 (Glen Rock, N.J.: Paulist Press, 1965), p. 75.

tizes, offers the eucharist and proclaims the Word of God. In the
assembly the Church accomplishes her work, which is to bring
scattered mankind back to unity and so build the body of Christ;[54]
the special fruit of the sacrifice, which is the climax of the assembly, is the unity of the body of Christ.[55] The Constitution on
the Sacred Liturgy, too, has every reason to remind us that the
apostolic works themselves are ordered to the liturgical assembly:[56] without it there is no Church.

On this basis we can understand the insistence of the Epistle
to the Hebrews and, later, of the Fathers of the Church, on
preaching fidelity in attending liturgical gatherings: "When you
gather often," writes Ignatius of Antioch, "the powers of Satan
are beaten down and his work of destruction ruined by the con-
cord of your faith." [57] And Hippolytus of Rome ends his exhor-
tation in the 35th chapter of the *Apostolic Tradition:* "Let each
also be sure to attend the assembly, for that is where the Holy
Spirit produces his fruit."

The unity in the forms of prayer, in the gestures of the cult
and in song is a sign of the unity in charity which the Holy Spirit
effects, but is also a means God uses to reenforce that unity and
charity and thereby strengthen the Church.[58] When she shows and
confesses that she is such as God has willed her, as the assembling
of men summoned together by the Word of God and answering
his call, the Church opens herself more and more to the grace of
her Lord who, seated at the right hand of the Father, sends her
the Spirit of the promise. In the assembly is prolonged the mystery of Pentecost, the term and crown of the paschal mystery.

[54] Cf. Chrysostom, *In 1 Cor.*, hom. 27, 3 (*P.G.* 61, col. 228).
[55] There are many texts in my book cited above, footnote 5, pp. 208-12.
[56] *Constitution on the Sacred Liturgy*, Art. 10.
[57] Ignatius, *Epist. ad Ephes.* 13, 1; cf. *Epist. ad Philad.* 6, 2.
[58] Clement of Rome, *Ad Cor.* 34, 7; Ignatius, *Ad Ephes.* 4, 1f.; Cyprian,
De Dominica Oratione 8 (ed. Hartel I, 271f.); Tertullian, *Apologeticum*
39, 2-4 (*Corp. Christ.* I, 150). For a general bibliography on the liturgical
assembly, see A. Martimort *et al., L'Eglise en prière. Introduction à la
liturgie* (Paris-Tournai, 1961), p. 82.

Ambroos-Remi van de Walle, O.P./*Louvain, Belgium*

How We Meet Christ in the Liturgical Community

The Constitution on the Sacred Liturgy and the liturgical renewal which it inaugurated will no doubt remain one of the most concrete and important results of Vatican Council II. But if this welcome renewal is not to harden sooner or later into a formalism more obstinate and destructive than that which we are now abandoning, it must be constantly accompanied by live theological thinking. This is not only vital for theology itself, since the liturgy is in fact a specific way of bringing about the presence of the reality of revelation in our human history, but it is just as vital for the life of the liturgy. For the liturgy must remain conscious and meaningful in its celebration; it must constantly replace ill-adjusted ways and means in a responsible manner, and it must remain constantly capable of incorporating new situations in new liturgical forms.

Revelation and the Church

If the celebration of the liturgy is to be meaningful, it can gain only by listening to the basic perspectives opened up by a rejuvenated theology. This theology has developed a new insight in the personal implications of our Christian existence. Formerly, Christians often looked on their relation with God as a "thing", an "object", something that was given shape in the believing acceptance of an "objective" truth, in the sense of something re-

19

vealed and imposed from outside; they passively submitted to a cult, rites and sacraments as autonomous, "thing"-like means of grace, and their morality consisted in a kind of blind obedience that made any personal decision of one's personal conscience superfluous. Today our theology sees the life of faith again, in genuine biblical fashion, as a *mutual* personal relationship between God and man, as a personal encounter, as a community of persons.

We have, in a certain sense, rediscovered revelation as an *event,* an *action,* in and through which God does not merely tell us a certain amount of unchangeable truths about himself and about our salvation, providing us with some means to work out this salvation, but in which he directly gives what he reveals and shares with us what he places before us. In this sense we certainly must continue to speak of an "objective" revelation, given and placed before us. What is revealed is the truth of a shared reality, one that is ultimately nothing else than the reality of the personal God himself. God gives himself to man in the Word, his Word, that became flesh and so entered within the historical dimensions of our own human existence. This he did in the man Jesus Christ who, as man, is the Son of God and who in this way, through his humanity, can give man a share in God's very own, personal life.

Man discovers and receives this gift of God in Christ in and through the act of faith. This "believing" does not arise on the basis of hearing somebody speak *about* God, but only through being moved inwardly *by* God. Only God can make us recognize God. This is precisely what happens when we believe. And so, the act of faith itself becomes part of the event of revelation insofar as God becomes present in man, insofar as we accept and, as it were, assimilate God as he gives himself. This gives birth to a relation of identity between revelation and faith, between revelation and Church. For the Church is the historical presence of God within our social dimensions, mediated for all time by the man Jesus, now glorified for all time. The Church is the believing community that has come about through God giving himself to man in Christ, in an action that remains eternally actual in history. The Church owes her being and continued realization to God acting in and through the glorified humanity of Christ, through which humanity is called to be the one People of God. The Church, then, is nothing else than the ostensible and tangible presence of God in history. She is in reality "the body of the Lord" on earth, the "root"-sacrament. Christ is truly present in the believing Church because faith is the way in which Christ shares himself in the historical present and lives in the faithful (cf. Eph. 3, 17).

Ecclesial Worship

The point of this brief theological sketch was to show that revelation and Church are one and that to believe is to establish a personal communion with the living God. It is not difficult to see how this basic fact leads to a better understanding of the true sense and function of the Church as a liturgical community. For liturgical worship is simply the realization of the Church at the point where she is most herself: the encounter with God in Christ. This is made real through the Lord who, in this meeting, extends his saving activity in the function exercised by the hierarchical ministers, and who, when received, is really present in the whole ecclesial community. And so, the Church realizes herself in and through liturgical worship; she thereby becomes more what she is, the People of God, the body of Christ on earth—and all this within human history.

The Church's liturgical worship is the worship of Christ himself in the Son's relationship to the Father, in and through the Church alive in his Spirit. It is nothing but the mediating, sacerdotal intercession of Christ with the Father for his Church, in and through his Church. For Christ did not simply institute liturgical worship in order to leave it to the hierarchy. He himself remains the real and primary subject of the Church's sacramental liturgy. In the hierarchical power of sanctification and mission, the Church only mediates and serves, but at the same time this service makes Christ sacramentally present in his actual redeem-

ing priesthood which establishes an immediate relationship between God and man. This is precisely the fruit of Christ's priestly
mediation, that in and through him we have direct access to the
Father (cf. Eph. 2, 13; 3, 13). In and through this priestly worship of Christ our relation to God, our prayer and our personal
worship are not merely made possible but become actual. Christ,
indeed, did not merely sacrifice himself *for* us but *in the name of
all of us.* Christ's worship *is* our very own worship. The Church's
sacramental liturgy simply makes Christ's own and supreme divine relationship real in us, so that it really "conforms" us for
the Father "to the image of his Son, that he should be the first-
born among many brethren" (Rom. 8, 29).

Christ lived this divine relationship as man, that is, on the
level of a creature, in filial obedience to the Father. It is in this
obedience-to-death to the will of the Father that Christ glorified
God and realized in a supreme manner the worship of God (cf.
John 17, 4). That is precisely why God glorified him too (cf.
Phil. 2, 5-11); that is how he became the source and cause of
our redemption (John 6, 38-40).

This worship of Christ was a worship in the name of all of us.
Any worship, any glorification that we offer to God and that
brings us glorification as it did to Christ, has already been
achieved in and through Christ and can, therefore, only be a
worship of participation in that offered by Christ on earth to the
Father and made eternal in heaven.

Insofar as the sacramental liturgy makes Christ's filial relation
to the Father actual, it is the means by which the Church is constituted a real liturgical community, that is, a community of
people with whom the Son shares his own relation to the Father,
and this is what the community celebrates. It is therefore not right
to see in the sacramental liturgy first of all, or exclusively, a
means of grace coming down from God to us. It is this, of course,
but only and precisely because of its value as worship, that is,
because of the divine relationship which Christ himself makes
actual and present in it and through which he inserts us into his
obedience, his love and his sacrifice and through which he ac-

quired glory for us. The sacraments that give us a "character" or mark also give us a share in Christ's priesthood, in his mediating glorification of God, and they make us capable of making Christ's divine relationship ours, each in his own function.

The Worship of the Faithful

Sacramental liturgy is, therefore, in the first place Christ's own activity, but in and through his Church which shares in this activity, and for that reason the Church exists as the community of the redeemed, a worshiping or liturgical community.

I have repeatedly emphasized that Christ offered his worship, and still offers it, in a lasting manner *in the name of all of us.* It is now our task to make this worship, this sacrifice, *ours* in the power of the Spirit. We must actively share in this worship. This is what we do in and through the Church's sacramental liturgy, the worship of Christ's community, the community of Head and members. For the liturgy is the worship of the Church as a community, as a whole. It never is the action of the isolated individual because it is, in the first place, the worship offered and continued by Christ himself in the name of *all,* as Head of a new humanity, the Church. Christ did not sacrifice himself as an individual but as the *caput humanitatis,* the Head of the human community. Through this sacrificial worship Christ not only made us children of the Father, but also brothers, one of another. In, through, and around the Word-made-flesh the Father gathered us all together in one faith, one hope, one love. We have become one people, that is, a congregation of people who, answering one and the same call, enact their inward and personal bond visibly and historically and therefore necessarily express it in an outward and historically observable fashion, in social activity; this also implies essentially an outward and communal worship.

We cannot reach God except in and through Christ, insofar as we belong to his body and constitute this body together with others. God only gives himself to us in Christ, and we meet Christ only within the believing community. Outside the Church

we simply do not exist for God in a personal community with
him. Outside the Church we are "no people" (cf. 1 Peter 2, 10),
and it is only *in* the Church that we come to exist for him and
through him.

What else is implied in the statement that the liturgy is the
worship of the Church as such? Nothing, except that the ecclesial community makes Christ's worship its own. Through the
mediating service of the hierarchical priesthood, Christ's worship,
glorifying God and sanctifying us, becomes present in a sacramental and visible manner for the salvation of the whole community. This becoming present, visible and actual is, from
Christ's point of view, nothing new or nothing more than his
sacrificial consent, eternally actual, for the community and in
the name of all. What is new can only be from the point of view
of the celebrating community which makes Christ's worship its
own in virtue of Christ's worship itself, *ex opere operato.* What is
new, what is more, what is special lies in the active participation
of the Church in the sacrificial worship of Christ, in the *opus
operantis Ecclesiae.* This itself is the fruit of the *opus operatum,*
the sacramental presence of Christ's worship. It is, indeed, as
has already been said, Christ's sacrifice that gives us access to
the Father, not only as a *possibility,* but as a *reality;* yet, the
personal, free and conscious relationship to God in Christ is
truly *our own.*

The sacramental presence we might call the invitation, the
astounding offer of Christ's mystery of redemption which is a
mystery of worship, but it is we ourselves who must freely accept
it, and accept it totally with the help of Christ's grace in us. And
this is what we do through faith, hope and love, the three facets
of man's total personal relationship to God. Without this personal
relationship, this free entering into Christ's divine relationship,
the merely objective presence of Christ's mystery has no religious
meaning whatever. Christ himself could work no wonders in
Nazareth because of the unbelief of his fellow citizens (cf. Mark
6, 5-6); neither can the Church, nor the liturgy, nor the sacraments. We cannot possibly attribute magical force to the sac-

ramental liturgy. It is true that the sacraments work *ex opere operato* but this is because they are an *opus operantis Christi;* in no sense does this mean that the sacraments work "automatically". We are redeemed as human beings, not as things that God manipulates as he likes. God appeals to our freedom; he himself sets our freedom moving. Every liturgical celebration, therefore, demands an active, personal relationship, if it is to have any meaning at all.

It is true that, outside this active faith of those who are present at the celebration, the liturgy is still offered to the Father as Christ's very own worship in and through the faith of the Church as such, insofar as those present take part at least intentionally. But insofar as those present are concerned, and this includes the celebrating priest, the meaning of this sacramental worship is determined by their active personal commitment, which is itself the firstfruit of the liturgical celebration.

When we talk of the liturgy as the Church's worship, there is a genuine danger that we may think of the Church as some personification, something real apart from the people who make up the Church and constitute the ecclesial community. The Church is, no doubt, more than the sum total of individual members, because she is the body of Christ, has Christ as Head and is animated by the Spirit. But it is precisely as Head that Christ makes the individual members into a community, and the Spirit lives in this community of people. And so, as the Church's communal worship, the liturgy must constantly be borne by the faith of the members of this community.

The liturgy, then, is Christ's worship which becomes ours insofar as we associate ourselves with the Church's faith in a total, personal relationship. The outward appearance of the liturgical celebration must therefore always be the outward, concrete and fully human expression of an inward worship, and this inward worship consists in associating oneself with the disposition with which Christ himself offers his worship to the Father: a disposition of obeying love. This is the way in which Christ glorifies the Father, and it is this glorification which the Church must per-

petuate historically and visibly. This is what makes the Church
the kingdom of God on earth, the kingdom in which God's total
sovereignty and majesty are recognized and made real, where
God is accepted as the beginning and end of all existence, where
all men and all things are treated as wholly God's in such a way
that they are not treated otherwise than according to God's purpose: in short, the kingdom where we let God be really God.
This is, in the end, the only worship God asks of us, and it is the
only spiritual worship which behooves us. It consists in nothing
but the extension of Christ's worship in such a way that it em-
braces the total scope of our human existence, with all that this
implies.

At this point, what we said about the unity of revelation and
the Church as the believing community shows some consequences
that we cannot avoid. We can no longer regard the sacraments
as if they were "things", as means of grace outside ourselves,
and in this sense looked at as "objects" with their own autonomous values. The sacraments are effective, meaningful signs
through which the glorified Christ meets us, simply for the sake
of meeting us. Sacraments are not things, but events or happen-
ings in which Christ gives himself to us in the various situations
of our pilgrimage. But even in this offer of sacramental grace
we meet Christ only in and through faith, by which this grace
becomes an inner reality, is accepted, is made present and makes
the living God real within us. Without this personal surrender
in faith through which we receive Christ, sacramental worship
simply has no *raison d'être*. The claim that the "Church's faith"
would still give meaning to this sacramental celebration without
the personal faith of the celebrating community can only rest
on a depersonalization of this "Church's faith", on the image of
a Church that is not constituted by its members, a Church that
is nothing but a "salvation institute" and not itself the saving
reality in and among the people that constitute it. We should
therefore constantly emphasize that the faith of the Church and
our personal faith are one because without this personal faith

of the members there simply is no Church and thus no bringing about of Christ's worship in history.

Even within the sacramental action, this encounter with God is an encounter of persons. In the sacraments, too, God speaks to man in Christ and calls upon man to go where he wants to lead him. They are both a gift and a mission, a question and an answer in unison: a powerless question prompted by man's lack of redemption and the all-powerful answer of God's redeeming love. Sacramental grace, therefore, does not stand apart from justification by faith. Both are tuned in on each other and cannot exist without each other.

Eucharistic Worship

All I have said about sacramental worship as the action of the liturgical community finds its climax in and through eucharistic worship. The whole liturgy finds its goal and center in the eucharist. "The eucharist is the goal and fulfillment of all the sacraments; it contains Christ himself who actually embodies the fullness of the priesthood." [1] It is in the eucharist that the Church is made fully real as the presence of God on earth within one community. This was emphasized during the Council: "Baptism constitutes the sacramental bond of unity existing among all who through it are reborn. But baptism, of itself, is only a beginning, a point of departure, for it is wholly directed toward the acquiring of fullness of life in Christ. Baptism is thus ordained toward a complete profession of faith, a complete incorporation into the system of salvation such as Christ himself willed it to be, and, finally, toward a complete integration into eucharistic communion." [2]

"In the sacrament of the eucharistic bread the unity of all believers who form one body in Christ (cf. 1 Cor. 10, 17) is both expressed and brought about." [3] "Really partaking of the

---

[1] St. Thomas, *Summa Theol.* III, 9.63, a.5.

[2] *Decree on Ecumenism* (text with commentary by Thomas Stransky, Glen Rock, N.J.: Paulist Press, 1965), n. 20, p. 80.

[3] *The Constitution on the Church* (text with commentary by Gregory Baum, Glen Rock, N.J.: Paulist Press, 1965), n. 3, p. 65.

body of the Lord in the breaking of the eucharistic bread, we are taken up into communion with him and with one another." [4] All this is really only a rewording of the very expressions of the New Testament and of a constant theological tradition.

At the Last Supper Christ accepted his death as a surrender to God, for us and in our name, and in this way anticipated sacramentally the redemption of the world, the establishment of the New Covenant in his blood, and so the establishment of the ecclesial community; it is *in this situation* that he gave himself to his disciples in the symbolic action of the Passover meal.

According to Scripture—in the institution narratives and in 1 Corinthians 11, 26—the eucharist is a proclamation of the death of the Lord. It is the *anamnesis,* the "memorial", of the meal at which the New Covenant, the Church, became a reality. It is through this eucharist that the Church is constantly made real in the world throughout history.

The same scriptural evidence makes it plain that the words "this is my body", and "this is my blood", cannot be taken in isolation from the rest. The words "take and eat—take and drink" are equally constitutive elements for this sacrament. Therefore, this sacrament also demands an active participation in the *sacrificial death* of Christ under the form of a *meal,* because it is quite definitely a getting-involved in the body that is *delivered up* and the blood that is *shed* for the remission of sins. It is, therefore, the death as surrender, as the supreme act of worship, which is directly and immediately made present through the sacramental sign in the form of a meal. This is precisely why Christ's body and blood are offered as food and drink. The eucharist is thus a meal *ratione sacramenti, i.e.,* in virtue of what it specifically signifies as a sacrament. It is in and through this meal that the glorified Christ wants to make the eternal actuality of the historical actions of his redemption into a personal redeeming event for those who continue his "cult", that is, his worship, for the Church.

[4] *Ibid.,* n. 7, p. 70.

Thus the eucharist too is primarily concerned with the active, dynamic presence of the glorified Lord, with a "present-making" *action* through which Christ involves the faithful in his *Passover,* his obedient surrender to the Father *and* his being accepted in glory by the Father. The final term of the eucharistic celebration, like that of any liturgical act of worship, is, therefore, the Father.

In the light of this purely scriptural perspective, we should explain the real presence of Christ in this sacrament. On the basis of his sacrificial death made present sacramentally, the Lord himself becomes present, and not the other way around, as if the Lord becomes present through the sacramental actualization of his sacrificial death. It is Christ's sacrificial death that is made present, that is, a real cult *event* or *happening,* and not so much a static form of Christ divorced from his deed of redemption.

The encounter with Christ in the eucharistic reality, therefore, signifies a concrete involvement in his paschal transition to the Father, a participation in his sacrifice in order to partake in his glorification. This is the supreme realization, the very crown of our Christian existence. Through it the ecclesial community becomes in a concrete manner the body of the Lord in which we meet one another in the heart of the Father, and through which we receive the one Spirit of the glorified Christ so that we can become a real witness to him in the world.

Therefore, it is imperative that we continue to understand the eucharist as a sacrament, as a sign of a signified reality directly brought about in this sacrament. The encounter with Christ in the eucharist is a real molding of the Church: "Because the bread is one, we though many, are one body, all of us who partake of the one bread" (1 Cor. 10, 17). By eating the eucharistic bread we all become members of this one body (cf. 1 Cor. 12, 27). "So we, the many, are one body in Christ, but severally members one of another" (Rom. 12, 5).

The eucharist remains the sign of this unity which it brings about and in which it finds the fulfillment of its meaning. This biblical approach to the eucharist will help us to maintain the right emphasis in this "mystery of the faith" and also to react selectively in our practical approach to this mystery.

We have already seen that the meaning of the institution of this sacrament lies primarily—in virtue of the sacramental sign itself—in the partaking of the sacrificial meal by which we are taken up actively in Christ's paschal transition to the Father. The eucharist is primarily the sacrament of Christ's Passover; its main purpose is not to be exposed, carried about, looked at or adored. All this, no doubt, is most meaningful and a consequence of the real presence which the Church can never doubt. The Dutch hierarchy, therefore, rightly declared in their Lenten pastoral of February 5, 1962: "The veneration of the blessed sacrament as such is linked too strongly with the very essence of the eucharist to consider it as something extra and unimportant." Yet, these eucharistic pious practices must remain or be guided in the right direction, and they should never be allowed to obscure the true meaning of this sacrament. The sacrament was not instituted by Christ with himself as the final term, but so that we could meet the Father in him through a total surrender to his divine will and so be glorified by him. Eucharistic piety, in whatever form, must always be a sacrificial devotion, a devotion of surrender to the Father in, through and with Christ. It must, therefore, always be a *communion,* a spiritual nourishing of the sacrificial will, a *votum sacramenti, i.e.,* a desire for the meaning, the reality, of the eucharistic, sacramental communion.

The unity of the Church and revelation is nowhere more clearly shown than in the reality of the eucharist. This reality is concerned with God's self-communication in Christ for the formation and building up of the Church. In the eucharist Christ gives himself and is present in his Church as the crucified and glorified Lord, as a tangible reality. In the eucharist the unity of the faithful with Christ and with each other is made most real and tangible. This sacrament of unity in Christ is the sacrament of love because, through it, we are taken into the heart of the Father and, in and with his Spirit, we begin to love all men as he loved the world. The liturgical community is a community of love by its very nature because it is a community formed in and by Christ, the Father's love made flesh, and together with the Father the source of the Spirit who is love.

The mystery of Christ's sanctifying worship in and through his Church becomes the expression of God's condescending, generous love in Christ Jesus, of the Church's bridal love and of the *believing* man who leaves his self and reaches beyond his self. The sacrifice is the line where all these levels intersect, but the encounter is fulfilled in the glory of the Lord. *Facie ad faciem te mihi, Christe, demonstrasti, in tuis te invenio sacramentis:* "Thou hast shown thyself to me in Christ, and thou I meet in thy sacraments." [5]

[5] E. Schillebeeckx, *Christ: The Sacrament of the Encounter with God* (New York: Sheed and Ward, 1963).

Casiano Floristán/*Madrid, Spain*

The Assembly and Its Pastoral Implications

Study of the assembly is one of the most apostolically far-reaching aspects of the present renovation of the pastoral aspect of the liturgy. Yet only recently has the theme been studied, beginning about fifteen years ago with the work of French liturgists, Martimort in particular.[1] Their first concern has been to place the liturgical concept of the assembly in its historical setting.

More recently, R. Gantoy[2] and Thierry Maertens[3] have made important contributions from a biblical approach, and Maertens' strictly biblical considerations have far-reaching pastoral consequences. The theology of the assembly has naturally been ap-

[1] A. Martimort, "L'assemblée liturgique," in *La Maison-Dieu* 20 (1950), pp. 153-75; "L'assemblée liturgique, mystère du Christ," *ibid.* 40 (1954), pp. 5-29; "Dimanche, assemblée et paroisse," *ibid.* 57 (1959), pp. 56-84; "Précisions sur l'assemblée," *ibid.* 60 (1959), pp. 7-34; "La asamblea," in *La Iglesia en oración: Introducción a la liturgia* (Barcelona: Herder, 1964), pp. 115-45. Cf. H. Chirat, *L'assemblée chrétienne à l'âge apostolique* (Paris, 1949); N. Afanasieff, "Le sacrement de l'assemblée," in *Internationale kirchliche Zeitschrift* (1956), pp. 200-13; J. Gelineau, "Nature et caractéristiques de l'assemblée chrétienne dans ses différentes formes," in *Problèmes d'assemblées* (Paris, 1961).

[2] R. Gantoy, "La asamblea en la economía de la salvación," in *Asambleas del Señor: Introducción* I (Madrid), pp. 56-82.

[3] T. Maertens, *La asamblea cristiana. De la liturgia bíblica a la pastoral del siglo XX* (Madrid, 1964). See also K. Schidt, "Ekklesia," in *Theologisches Wörterbuch zum Neuen Testament* III (Stuttgart, 1938), pp. 502-39.

proached also from the standpoint of ecclesiology, particularly in the work of P. Tena.[4] But despite the advances made in ecclesiology in recent years, the assembly has not been given the place it deserves in treatises on the nature of the Church.[5]

In pontifical documents the word "assembly" seldom appeared before the Constitution on the Sacred Liturgy. It did not even occur in the *Instructio* of September 3, 1958, and only recently has it appeared in liturgical manuals.[6] And yet it is an evident fact in the New Testament and the Fathers, a fact of worship from the earliest times, as any liturgical historian can see.

I do not propose here to embark on a biblical, liturgical or patristic study of the assembly, but rather to examine its sociological conditioning with a view to setting down some thoughts on its pastoral importance.

1. *The Assembly as the Principal "Sign" of the Church*

Of all the liturgical "signs", the assembly is the most important and the oldest. Hence, it is the principal sign of the Church. Historians and theologians of the assembly begin by studying the Jewish *Qahal*. The assembly of the People of God is a reunion-in-worship, convoked by God for the good of its participants. The history of Israel, which began as a people organized in the assembly in the wilderness, is studded with successive assemblies, up till the assembly of all the nations. Before expressing a liturgical reality, the assembly is an ecclesial reality.

The second definitive moment of the assembly is the convocation made by Jesus Christ. The person of the Lord as the glorious risen *Kyrios* is the center of the new Christian assembly. The New Testament assembly calls everyone without distinction

---

[4] P. Tena, *La palabra "ekklesia". Estudio histórico-teológico* (Barcelona, 1958). Cf. also M. Useros, "Eclesiología y pastoral de la asamblea," in *Sal Terrae* 53/7 (1965).

[5] The same could be said of works dealing with the parish. The assembly does not occupy the central position in any of these. Cf. my book *La Parroquia, comunidad eucarística* (Madrid, 1964). See the bibliography at the end.

[6] The following liturgical works study the assembly: L. Bouyer, *La vie de la liturgie;* R. Paquier, *Traité liturgique;* I. Dalmais, *Initiation à la liturgie;* G. Vagaggini, *El sentido teológico de la liturgia.*

of race. It is not an end, but a beginning—a sign of the nascent history of the Church. If the Christian people come together every Sunday, it is to call again those who are still absent.

In the early Church the assembly was the reason for the celebration of the Word and the Sacrament through the love in Christian hearts (Acts 2, 42-45). The *Didachē* and St. Justin confirm this.

The reunion of Christians each Sunday has always been not merely the best manifestation of the Church, but also the source and culmination of her whole pastoral activity. The mystery of Christ is realized in the liturgy as in no other activity of the Church. Therefore, the liturgical ministry has always been the most important apostolic task.[7]

2. *The Assembly and the Threefold Pastoral Office*

The domain of pastoral activity is the same as that of the Church, as much in her communities as in her relationship with the world.[8] In the final analysis, it is the Savior's work in his epiphany, paschal sacrifice and sending of the Holy Spirit.

Pastoral activity has traditionally been divided into three parts: the prophetic ministry, including the *munus docendi;* the liturgical ministry, including the *munus sanctificandi;* and the day-to-day ministry, including the *munus regendi.*

The assembly, especially the eucharist, is at the heart of the

[7] Cf. M. Lohrer, "Die Feier des Mysteriums der Kirche: Kulttheologie und Liturgie der Kirche," in *Handbuch der Pastoraltheologie* I (Freiburg i. Br.), pp. 287-332; A. Verheul, *Einführung in die Liturgie* (Vienna, 1964). An English translation is in preparation, entitled *Introduction to the Liturgy.* Cf. also the *Constitution on the Sacred Liturgy,* Arts. 2, 26, 33, 41, and 42.

[8] Cf. F. Arnold, "Was ist Pastoraltheologie?" in *Wort des Heils als Wort in die Zeit* (Trier, 1961), pp. 296-300; M. Pfliegler, *Pastoraltheologie* (Vienna, 1962); *Handbuch der Pastoraltheologie* I (Freiburg i. Br., 1964); Guy de Bretagne, *Pastorale fondamentale* (Bruges, 1964); H. Denis, "Vertiente pastoral del estudio de la Teología," in *Seminarios* 14 (1961), pp. 81-109; 15 (1961), pp. 71-99; P. A. Liégé, "Introduction," in F. Arnold, *Al servicio de la fé* (Barcelona, 1963); *Problemas actuales de Pastoral* (1st International Congress at Fribourg, 1961) (Madrid, 1963); G. Ceriani, *Introduzione alla Teologia Pastorale* (Vicenza, 1961); *Apostolic Renewal in the Seminary* (New York: The Christophers, 1965).

liturgical ministry. Therefore, one can speak of pastoral activity "anterior" to the liturgy: the prophetic ministry or the task of transmitting the Word of God to awaken or increase faith. Those who are to be called to the liturgy must first be called to faith and conversion (Constitution on the Sacred Liturgy, Art. 9). Evangelization and catechesis must precede the liturgical ministry, and all evangelization and catechesis has the aim of making men participating members of the assembly (Constitution on the Sacred Liturgy, Art. 9).

There is also pastoral activity "posterior" to the liturgy. The whole of Christian life is the continuous practice of charity. The liturgy is the glory of God and the sanctification of mankind at the same time. What has been lived in the liturgical celebration—the charity of Christ in the Church—must be lived in all men and in their communities.

This "before" and "after" should not be taken in a chronological, but a logical sense. The prophetic ministry, which logically, psychologically and temporally precedes the liturgical ministry, coincides, in actual time, with the day-to-day ministry, since all time outside that of the liturgical celebration is at once before and after the assembly.

In the assembly, the principal sign of the Church and of the liturgy, the signs of worship are manifested, and these can only be understood by those who have faith. The pastoral aspect of the liturgy of the assembly revolves around various signs of worship. But men are not converted, and so they will not come to the assembly without entering into contact with the divinity through other religious signs, not of worship, but of mission. The first of these are the signs of charity, the most constant and universal signs visible to humanity. They will be signs of a charity that is not only heroic but transcendental. The Christian signs of charity are full of the Word of God as a prophetic Word, preceding and following the rite of worship. The Word of God— at least in intention—makes the signs of charity effective in a natural way in the Church, that is, in the whole of Christian life, just as it makes the signs of worship effective in a sacramental way (*ex vi verborum*). So there are two great signs of the Church:

(a) Signs of *charity* outside the assembly, the expression of natural worship.

(b) Signs of *worship* inside the assembly, the perfect expression of the mystery of Christ and the Christian *agape*.

The pastoral aspect of the liturgy of the assembly is at the heart of all pastoral activity. Both the ministry of evangelization and catechesis and the ministry which shows the signs of charity will exercise their mission in a Christian manner if they take the assembly as their point of departure and the goal of their endeavors.

3. *The Assembly and Human Society*

Pastoral study of the assembly cannot be confined to a biblical or liturgical study. Maertens and Martimort both give magnificent pastoral guidance drawn from Scripture,[9] but the findings of sociology are also needed. Ecclesiology will be a principal starting point for a contemporary pastoral examination, but not the only one.[10] A study based on the nature of the Church, if it is to be truly pastoral in outlook, needs an examination of the actual situation in that this is a moment in the history of salvation. Pastoral theology is the branch of theology that analyzes concrete situations, in the light of which its structure is developed. Its principles will always be theological, whether dealing with an internal or external analysis of the Church.

Therefore, a pastoral analysis of the assembly, the principal sign of the Church, requires theological criteria, since the reality under analysis is not merely profane, but mysterious. But at the same time, the thoughts of the pastoral theologian and the action of the pastor must take account of the facts brought to light by sociological and psychological observations of the assembly as a reunion of religious men and women. If the sociologist's and

[9] Particularly in "Précisions sur l'assemblée," in *La Maison-Dieu* 60 (1959), pp. 7-34.

[10] Arnold in Germany and Liégé in France are the pastoral theologians who have gone deepest into the ecclesiological significance of ecclesial actions.

psychologist's criteria of analysis are attuned to the principles and requirements of the pastoral ministry, their observations will be extremely valuable to those who exercise this ministry. Although it is for the pastoral theologian, not the sociologist, to trace out a pastoral theology of the assembly, he will be helped by the sociologist (and theologians of other disciplines) who will provide criteria for a real meeting of theology and sociology and not a mere juxtaposition of facts derived from revelation on one side and the concrete situation on the other.[11]

Religious sociology has been much discussed in the last twenty-five years from sociographic, morphological, formal and theoretical or psycho-social points of view.[12] However, sociological examination of the assembly itself is more recent.[13]

It is clear that God does not bestow sanctification or salvation

[11] Cf. the basic work by F. Arnold, "Das gottmenschliche Prinzip der Seelsorge," in *Seelsorge aus der Mitte der Heilsgeschichte* (Freiburg, 1956), pp. 16-62.

[12] Thought-provoking, if not strictly sociological, are the works of G. Le Brass, *Etudes de sociologie religieuse* I-II (Paris, 1955-6). They originated a tendency which Carrier has called "religious morphology". My doctoral thesis *La vertiente pastoral de la sociología religiosa* (Vitoria, 1960) studied the socio-religious school of Le Brass. A second school has been formed, mainly by German "formalist" authors such as G. Mensching, *Soziologie der Religion* (Bonn, 1947). The third school, of religious "psychosociology", is the most interesting from the pastoral aspect. The main works are those of F. Houtart, E. Pin and H. Carrier. Cf. particularly the latter's *La Psycho-sociologie de l'appartenance religieuse* (Rome, 1960).

[13] Cf. J. Fichter, *Southern Parish: I. Dynamics of a City Church* (Chicago: Univ. of Chicago Press, 1951); *Social Relations in the Urban Parish* (Chicago: Univ. of Chicago Press, 1954); D. Goldschmidt, F. Greiner, H. Schelsky, *Soziologie der Kirchengemeinde in soziologischer Sicht* (Hamburg, 1959); E. Pin, *Introduction à l'Etude Sociologique des Paroisses Catholiques* (Paris, 1956); *Paroisses urbaines, paroisses rurales* (The 1956 Louvain Conference) (Paris, 1958); E. Pin, "Can the Urban Parish Be a Community?" in *Gregorianum* 41 (1960), pp. 393-423; "La sociologie de la Paroisse," in *Situation de la Paroisse* (The 1961 European Parish Colloquy) (Paris, 1962); F. Houtart, "Sociologie de la Paroisse comme assemblée eucharistique," in *Social Compass* 10/1 (1963) and "La paroisse se cherche," in *Biblica* (1963), pp. 111-25; N. Greinacher, "Soziologische Aspekte des Selbstvollzugs der Kirche," in *Handbuch der Pastoraltheologie* I, pp. 415-48; B. Häring, "Die gemeinschaftsbildene-kraft der Liturgie," in *Liturgisches Jahrbuch* 7 (1957), pp. 205-14; T. Rendtorpf, *Die soziale Struktur der Gemeinde* (Hamburg, 1958).

on man "in general" but on man as an individual in a particular situation. The Christian vocation involves the whole man in all of his social relationships; therefore all the facets and ages of man have to be christianized. Today, man's social and community consciousness has been awakened after perhaps three centuries of individualistic sleep. Since the end of World War II, not only has the concept of a social Christianity gained ground, but man's innermost relations to God have gained a new dimension of involvement with his fellowmen.[14]

The assembly is a special case of the religious involvement of a group of believers in communication with the Godhead. The personal efficacy of the assembly is, without doubt, very relevant today, thanks to man's discovery of a profound social and community sense both within and without the Church. A Christianity without the idea of assembly would be catastrophic today, since it would be attempting to swim against the tide of secular history—which is always a "trace" of God—and of the history of salvation.

In order to undertake a sociological examination of the assembly, we must first ask the theologian what he understands by the idea of "assembly". Gantoy defines it as "a community lawfully convoked and presently assembled in order to hear the Word of God, to pray with the whole Church and to celebrate the eucharistic sacrifice, waiting for the return of the Lord who has come and will come again".[15]

Early analyses of religious sociology have tended to examine the morphology, or structural characteristics, of the Sunday eucharistic assembly, concentrating more on each individual in it than on the group as a whole. The reason for this is perhaps that statistics have often been compiled by priests full of zeal but lacking in sociological training.

A second class of observations would reveal that the parish— and hence its nucleus, the assembly—is not a group but simply

[14] Cf. M.-D. Chenu, "La révolution communitaire et l'apostolat," in *La Parole de Dieu II: L'Evangile dans le temps* (Paris, 1964), pp. 363-78.
[15] R. Gantoy, *op. cit.,* p. 60.

a social system.[16] Its members are not bound by any common aim; they have no deep feelings of solidarity with one another, nor, in many cases, with their clergy; they include many spectators who merely happen to be together while following their individual pious devotions; they have no particular needs which depend on group action; the place where they come together, the place of worship, often has chapels that favor isolation and dispersal; the celebrant often has little sense of presiding over an assembly and rarely does the Sunday reunion indicate Christian criteria of behavior in the work or leisure group, in the family or in society. Knowledge of the findings of such an analysis (which need not of course be understood to include every assembly), made by sociologists using basic criteria derived from a true understanding of the nature of the Church, is absolutely necessary to the pastor of souls.

Christian life without the eucharistic assembly is impossible, since the eucharist is the privileged act by which the Church is shown forth and made present.[17] From the first sacrament, baptism, which gives us the right to attend a particular eucharistic assembly, to the liturgy of the dead, which celebrates a transit from a concrete assembly to the celestial assembly, the whole of the Christian's life is bound up—whether he realizes it or not—with the assembly.

From a pastoral point of view we must find answers to the following questions about the assembly:

1. Does each member of the assembly feel he *belongs?* Naturally, when the liturgy lacks life, reality and communication, there can be no real feeling of belonging. Somehow all must be convinced that they cannot receive the fullness of grace without the assembly.[18]

[16] Cf., for example, B. Wicker, "The Ministry of the Word," in *New Blackfriars* (Nov. 1965), to be reprinted in *The Mass and the People of God* (London: Burns & Oates; New York: Herder and Herder, 1966).

[17] J. Frisque, "Participation à l'Eucharistie et appartenance à l'Eglise," in *Biblica* (1963), pp. 129-39.

[18] F. Houtart, following Fichter, holds that the assembly is a "congregation" and not a "group", since there is physical proximity and social communication through common participation, but no continuity is needed

2. How *active is the participation* of each member in the assembly? (Constitution on the Sacred Liturgy, Arts. 11, 14, 19, 21, 26, 48.) When the individuals who make up a group are conscious of their affiliation to the group and take an active part in it, they form a "community". The formation of a community mentality must be one of the most specific tasks of anyone responsible for the assembly.

3. How *hierarchical* should the structure of each Christian assembly be? The assembly is a "sacrament" of unity, a "holy people brought together and organized under the direction of the bishop" (Constitution on the Sacred Liturgy, Art. 26). Within the assembly there is a series of "services"—in the sanctuary or the nave—to be performed in unison by all members. The danger of "clericalizing" the assembly, or of a priest, particularly a bishop, celebrating without a sense of community, is evident.

4. How *universal* or *catholic* is the assembly in its composition? The assembly is not based on respect of persons, nor is it a great human privilege (1 Cor. 12, 13; Gal. 3, 28). Neither is the assembly made up of the "pure" or of a limited circle of the devout; it is especially open to sinners so that it can perform its work of sanctification in them (Constitution on the Sacred Liturgy, Art. 32).

5. Does the assembly perform a *pastoral* service, initiating and strengthening the faith of its members? The liturgical assembly is not the Church's only field of activity, but it does require instruction to go with it in order to bring new members to the sacramentary acts of initiation and all its members to maturity in faith and charity.

6. How *suitable* is the *place* of worship? The place of worship is called a church, the same word that is used of the community assembled in it. But, as the feeling has been lost sight of that it is not the place, but the assembly of people in it that is the more important, so the mere edifice of dead stones instead of

---

among those who constitute each assembly. The assembly is not just a group, since this does not necessarily imply physical proximity.

the temple of living stones has sometimes been dignified by the use of a capital letter and is referred to as the "Church". The building is normally the reflection of the life of worship of the assembly; the architectural history of the Christian Church is a crystallization of the history of liturgical celebration. From the sociological point of view, it is important to decide where the best place to build a church is, and what shape it should take.

7. What are the *relations* between the *assembly* and the *broader human community?* In a rural society it is fairly natural for the assembly to correspond to the basic human community. But when the structure of the human community changes, particularly in the city, the structure of the Christian assembly must change with it.

First, there must be several liturgical assemblies in a city because the Church is a local event. But the eucharistic assembly is preceded by the baptismal assembly, and this by the assembly of catechumens. From a pastoral point of view it is not necessary for every place of worship in a city to be constructed on the usual baptismal font — altar axis. This involves a new concept of urban pastoral work. The city-dweller is becoming progressively less bound up with his street and district and feels himself to be more and more a part of the whole city community. And so, just as local government is being organized on a progressively wider basis so that whole cities or metropolitan areas are under one council, pastoral organization must also adapt itself to the urban scale, linking the work of the eucharistic assemblies with baptismal assemblies and catechetical groups.[19]

8. What is the relationship between the *parochial* assembly and the *diocesan* assembly? The life of the Church does not go on only at parish level, since the parish is a "participation" in the local Church. On the other hand, this local Church, presided over by the bishop, is a "concentration" of the whole Church in one place. A true collegiality of parochial assemblies under the direction of the bishop must be established and developed, just

[19] Cf. C. Floristán, "Misión, Liturgia y Parroquia," in *Pastoral Misionera* 1 (1965), pp. 22-38.

as the diocesan assembly must live in a collegial sense on the ecumenical and catholic level of the whole Church. The bishop, as a member of the episcopal college presided over by the pope, sums up in his person the eucharistic and sacramental ministry of the Christian assembly and the prophetic and charitable ministry of the different evangelizing groups.

4. *Conclusion*

In the current pastoral revival, the assembly is of crucial importance. As a sign of the Church it reveals the whole community dimension of the People of God, and as a liturgical sign it shows the situation of the People of God as protagonists in salvation history. The threefold work of pastoral activity (prophetic, liturgical and day-to-day) refers to the assembly; the Christian advancement of the assembly is likewise the ultimate aim of all human advancement, since the kingdom of heaven, the place of rest for all those who work temporally in the kingdom of the first creation, is compared in the Bible to a wedding feast—and this is made present, although under the veil of symbols, in each meeting of the eucharistic assembly.

The Christian assembly cannot be improvised; it requires continuous and detailed preparation. The activities of its members must be *prepared* in advance and each of its celebrations must be revised. The assembly does not meet to "comply with" a juridical precept, but rather to make present the paschal event which brings salvation to men. The ever-threatening temptation to mechanical repetition must be avoided, and this requires that at each epoch of time the celebration must be sufficiently "new" for everyone to take part full of expectation. Although the assembly lives in anticipation of the mysterious reality of a liturgy which foreshadows the life of heaven, it must never lose sight of the fact that it is temporal, that it breaks up every time it comes together, because it is essentially missionary and the time of mission is not yet at an end. Therefore, the assembly provides real human problems with an answer deduced from the divine mysteries. This answer will be effective when it ceases to be standard, when those responsible for it—particularly the celebrant—know how to break the sacred silence with necessary words and when each one of its members receives the message of Christ as though it were directed to him alone. Those who serve the assembly will attend to the welcome of those who come to it; the notices will each time be carefully prepared so as to be those most suitable to that particular reunion; the homily will be a true proclamation of the wonders of God, inspired by the sacred texts and in harmony with the mystery that is being celebrated and the particular needs of the congregation; the musical chants will help the people to profess their Christianity in accordance with the lyrical genius of their particular culture; the prayers of the faithful will embody the events in their lives that are foremost on the day of the assembly; the postures of the faithful will help all to participate actively, consciously and fully in the activity inherently required of them by the liturgy.

We are still a long way from the ideal liturgical assembly.[20] Most of our eucharistic assemblies are still lacking in life; they neither relate to the problems of life nor do they show a strong inner cohesion. Yet, the hour of the Christian assembly has struck. Precisely because the assembly of the Council has produced such evidence of vitality and such great fruits of renovation, we are led to hope that on the episcopal level of all the priests in a diocese, and on the level of the shared local assembly, the Church will show in present-day history the youthful strength of her message of salvation that the world cannot give.

[20] If the liturgical laws allowed it, how many priests would be capable of celebrating the eucharist with just a Bible and some bread and wine, simply following the guidance of tradition? Experience has shown that there are very few who can even improvise well a concluding prayer for the Prayer of the Faithful.

Helmut Hucke/*Neu-Isenburg, W. Germany*

Musical Requirements of Liturgical Reform

At first sight it may seem strange to write of the musical requirements of the liturgical reform. In the *Motu Proprio* "Tra le sollecitudini" of 1903, Pius X spoke of music as a "humble handmaid" (*umile ancella*) of the liturgy.[1] The Constitution on the Sacred Liturgy speaks of the role of music in the liturgy as a "ministerial function" (*munus ministeriale*).[2] Are there any requirements for church music, if it is to serve the liturgy? Are there any requirements for subordinating church music to the demands of the liturgy?

On this point it cannot be denied that music—and in this, it is like every other art form—is ruled from within by certain legitimate demands and laws. Are these legitimate demands and laws, which govern the inner, material nature of the prerequisites of the art form, irrelevant to the liturgy? Are they exclusively the concern of music? Are these requirements the concern solely of musicians in their solicitude for "true art"? Should not musicians in their own way have finished with these concerns when they offer their music to the service of divine worship?

In the last centuries, the relationship between liturgy and

[1] *Motu proprio "Tra le sollecitudini"*, § 23. In a letter from Cardinal Secretary of State Tardini to Cardinal Frings on the occasion of the Church Music Congress at Cologne, 1961, it is called *praecipua ancilla*. The letter is printed in the Minutes of the Congress, 4-5.
[2] Art. 112.

45

music in the Church consisted in the fact that liturgy made certain demands on church music, but otherwise left it alone. First and foremost, it was the duty of church music to give expression to the liturgical text in the Latin language.[3] Any other developments were looked upon with misgivings.[4] At times, and especially in more recent periods, certain guiding norms of a stylistic and historical nature were held up to church music.[5] But the real criterion for liturgical usefulness, if not entirely for the liturgical character of all music, was still the "liturgical" text in Latin. If the music simply adhered to this text, then fundamentally it enjoyed unlimited freedom and became a law unto itself. Any other offense—except one against the text—could be repaired. The text alone was seen to have a properly inherent musical and artistic importance.[6]

[3] Cf. A. Bugnini, *Liturgia Viva: Commento all'Instruzione della S.C. dei Riti sulla Musica sacra e la Liturgia, September 3, 1958* (Milan, 1962), pp. 73ff.

[4] Thus, the Sacred Congregation of Apostolic Visitation issued a decree in 1665: "Che non si canti a voce sola tanto grave, quanto acuto, tutto o parte notabile d'un salmo, inno o mottetto. . ." (reprinted by F. Romita, *Ius Musicae Liturgicae* [Turin, 1936], p. 80). This prohibition is aimed at the non-ecclesiastical tradition of singing recitative and arias in the church. The view of the legislators was, however, so much influenced by contemporary musical development that the solos of the cantors, which still constitute an essential part of Gregorian Chant, were not mentioned in so many words; according to the letter of the law, Gregorian responsories would also have fallen under this prohibition. How rigidly such principles, once established, were adhered to, is shown also in the *Instructio de Musica Sacra et Sacra Liturgia* of the Sacred Congregation of Rites (September 3, 1958). There it is laid down in n. 93c: "Laici vero masculini sexus . . . cum a competente auctoritate ecclesiastica . . . ad Musicam sacram exsequendam deputantur, si tale officium modo et forma a rubricis statutis peragant, servitium ministeriale directum quidem, sed delegatum, exercent, ea tamen condicione, si de cantu agatur, et chorum seu 'schola cantorum' constituant." Accordingly, no doubt, the laymen's *schola,* which sang the Gradual responsory, exercised a liturgical function, but not the lay cantor, who, according to the rubrics, should sing the Gradual verse!

[5] Especially "Der Gregorianische Gesang und die Musik Palestrinas," cf. Bugnini, *op. cit.,* pp. 46ff.; 50ff.

[6] Of course, it is especially in more recent times that an attempt has been made to have "church music style" conform to the regulations. The St. Cecilia Society has made the most significant efforts of this sort in the German-language area with its *Cäcilienvereins-Katalog.* But "so valuable have been the editions of classical polyphony and the many compositions

The first consequence was that, whereas formerly every word and every gesture in the liturgy had been fixed and rigid for centuries, the music of the liturgy (with the exception of the chants for the clergy) took on a wider development in keeping with changes in musical style and the growth of musical forms.[7] Hence there was scarcely any other development in the understanding of the liturgy in the last century so significant as in the history of church music. Church music was the medium by means of which the liturgy adapted itself to the period and to society. But such adaptation was possible only where the prerequisites were available and had a part in the art of church music. Where these prerequisites were not observed, the liturgy remained a *Missa lecta;* and where people were not satisfied with the prerequisites, only ersatz forms arose, like the German high Mass, the "sung Mass", a hymn at the end of Mass, and the Mass with organ accompaniment. By means of church music the court musicians were able to adapt the Church's liturgy to the social gatherings of middle class culture. And the text of the *Ordinary* of the Mass became a libretto not only for the composers of the Catholic Church, but it was generally considered as such: the most potentially musical libretto in the whole of the history of music, with challenges enough for every composer who wished to try his skill and demonstrate his power.

The liturgical reform would seem then, at a superficial glance, a very favorable occasion—and so it has been understood by some musicians—for giving church music a new lease on life: it would put words into the mouths of the people, and make it possi-

---

created in their spirit, so serious has become the official recognition of an enormous mass devoid of any artistic significance, frequently not even of decent, workmanlike compositions for use in the churches, which now cannot be considered competent as church music . . . Artistic merit has been subordinated to external liturgical correctness, one-sided judgment, and the adherence to the externals of such an ideal style, that musical poverty has brought the movement to a standstill." K. Fellerer, "Caecilianismus," in *Die Musik in Geschicte und Gegenwart,* II, pp. 623ff.

[7] J. Jungmann in his lecture "Kirchenmusik und Liturgiereform" in *Internationalen Studienwoche für Kirchenmusik* (Fribourg), 22 (August 28, 1965), has pointed this out. The lectures given during this study-week are being collected and will appear in German, French, English, Italian, and Spanish-language editions.

ble for them to sing. But if this were the only question, then it would be proper to ask whether the Church is not making a hasty capitulation to the prevailing mode of life in the current sociological structure. Have we not here a very great sacrifice to make, when the priceless heritage of centuries of church music is being called into question? Church music, like the Latin language, still enjoys some elements of universality, though it is, as far as genuine church music is concerned, here and there falling into decay, its real character as an art seriously jeopardized. A vapid musicianship, nothing more than a kind of "sing-along", stands ready and willing to step into its place in the liturgical structure.

But this will get us nowhere. The Constitution on the Sacred Liturgy asserts that church music will be "the more holy in proportion as it is more closely connected with the liturgical action".[8] It also understands church music as a function of the liturgical action. And it asserts further: in the liturgical renewal "texts and rites should be drawn up so that they express more clearly the holy things which they signify; the Christian people, so far as possible, should be enabled to understand them with ease and to take part in them fully, actively, and as befits a community".[9] But this demands that church music shall be treated not only as an apparatus to convey the loftiness and splendor of the Church's ceremonies, or as an alternative to speech for a part of the liturgical text; in itself it must also have the quality of ritual. For music is a sign; it is the most readily perceptible sign at the disposal of worship. But if the music of the liturgy is to be a sign, it must be understood and used otherwise than it has been up to now; the relationship, therefore, between liturgy and music must be changed and the whole structure rebuilt on a new and original foundation. Moreover, it is no longer enough for the liturgy to impose definite duties on church music and, for the rest, to let it go its own way, but it must in real earnest accept music in the church as an inherent function of the liturgy and as an integral component of the liturgy. Inasmuch as it is

[8] Art. 112.
[9] Art. 21.

considered to "have the character of a sign"—musical in nature and form—the liturgy must learn to use music as a language of signs. These are the musical premises of the liturgical reform.

Kinds of Singing

The concept of *singing,* in modern Western languages, includes very different kinds of "expressions-of-being-alive". We may think, perhaps, of the lullaby with which a mother sings her sick child to sleep, of tunes heard at a community songfest, of the aria of an opera singer, or of the soloist of a jazz band. These can all be called *singing;* in form, they may include humming to oneself, singing to someone else, calling out to somebody in a musical phrase. Therefore, it is idle to ask what is the origin of singing; we must rather ask after the origin of different kinds of singing.

We distinguish three fundamental types of singing:

1. *Recitative.* The characteristics of this form in the primitive tradition of worship, in contrast to *recitative* with instrumental accompaniment which, in the West, became the art form developed during the baroque period, have recently become acclimatized in the form of *chant.*

2. The *song,* or *cry,* or *summons,* and the response to it in unison (the *litany*), and the *acclamation,* also in unison.

3. *Singing,* properly so-called.

Chant[10]

The term *recitative* has two meanings. Thus, it is possible to recite on a fixed musical phrase, or in a free, "spoken" melody, which resists being forced into a musical system; therefore, it can be either *sung* or *spoken.* The sung recitative and the chant use typical models and turns, the application of which is more or less improvised. If the progress of the melody itself is fixed, there

[10] Cf. literature cited in *Concilium,* Vol. 2 (Glen Rock: Paulist Press, 1965), p. 133. Also: S. Corbin, "La cantillation des rituels chrétiens," in *Revue de Musicologie,* 47 (1961), pp. 3-36; W. Lipphardt, "Luthers Lesetöne," in *Musik und Altar,* 16 (1964), pp. 170-6; F. Schieri, "Die gesungene liturgische Lesung in deutscher Sprache: ein Vorschlag," *ibid.,* pp. 163-70, and 17 (1965), pp. 18-30.

still remain, nonetheless, the rhythm, the tempo and other factors within the structure of the performance, which are left to the discretion of the performer. On the basis of these improvised elements, chant is, by its nature, a solo performance. The chant forms are not absolutely fixed musical structures; they have their initial *raison d'être* in the text.

The object of the chant is not singing, not music, so much as it is the word. Singing is only the manner in which the word is expressed. Where the cantor is immeasurably or deeply affected by joy, by enthusiasm in the word or in the song, or by his own singing, so that the word is no longer preeminent, the chant breaks into a *jubilus* or a *glossolalia*. "He who rejoices," says St. Augustine, and this is the theology of the *jubilus*, "knows words no longer. Who is worthy of this *jubilus*, if not the ineffable God? And if you are not worthy of speaking to him and dare not be silent, what remains then but to shout for joy, that the heart should wordlessly exult and the measureless extent of your joy should overleap the limits of syllables?" [11]

Chant in the Liturgy[12]

Our liturgy makes use of chant when the Word of God is proclaimed to the community and when the celebrant offers to God the prayer of the whole liturgical assembly. The celebrant does not sing his personal prayer. Through the chant-formulas, the epistle and the official prayer—except in the case of concelebration and the solemn eucharistic prayers—are distinguished from other examples of the Word in the liturgy. The chant is a sign of the dialogue of the people and is more meaningful and more significant than any other action and every form of catechesis.

The reading is sung in a different manner from the prayer. Under the heading of "readings" come the psalm in the "service

---

[11] St. Augustine, *In Ps. 99* (*P.L.* 37, col. 1272), *In Ps. 32* (*P.L.* 36, col. 283). St. Paul describes *glossolalia* as "the prayer of the spirit" during which the understanding remains without fruit. "He that speaketh in a tongue, edifieth himself", 1 Cor. 14, 4.

[12] Cf. L. Agustoni, "La cantillazione delle letture e delle preghiere nella messa," in preparation. Cf. *supra*, footnote 7.

of the Word", the *psalmus responsorius,* and later, the (*respon-sorium*) *graduale,* which is another kind of chant. It is a literary genre in its own right after the manner of a song: a "sung" read-ing. The most important of these prayers are the solemn petitions, *e.g.,* the *Preface* and the *Pater Noster,* which are distinguished by another kind of chant.

In early times the chant had to foster the intelligibility of the words. This was not the least of its functions. A voice raised in chanting is more audible and better understood than when it is used simply to speak. Today when a man wishes to make himself understood in a large room or before a great crowd, he uses a microphone and a loudspeaker. And in most cultures men are no longer used to being addressed in song.

As long as readings and petitions were chanted in Latin, listen-ers were able to accept them in a foreign tongue as a tradition: the text was in any case stylized and strange to them because it was in a foreign language. But the translation of the text into the vernacular poses the question anew whether the text should be sung or spoken. Today, the chant is something outlandish, peculiar only to worship and immediately connected with it. In many present-day cultures hardly anyone chants in his mother tongue; in some vernaculars it does not occur at all.

Men in earlier times sang more than they do today, but they did not sing all the words. Daily communication and personal relationships cannot be carried on in song; if they are, conversa-tion becomes theater or parody.

The question whether man today should sing or speak is not to be decided in the same way for all cultures and for every lan-guage. And the question as it concerns reading and petition is not one question but two.

Chanted or Spoken Reading[13]

Undoubtedly the technical means now at our disposal open up not only new means but also new possibilities for the future

[13] J. Gelineau, "Faut-il chanter les lectures en français?" in *Eglise qui chante* (1964), pp. 55-6. In German: "Ist es notwendig, die lesungen in der landesprache zu singen?" in *Musik und Altar,* 16 (1964), pp. 145-9.

of proclamation. Thus, for example, the loudspeaker allows us to proclaim the Word in a very large room and before a larger assembly and in a more personal way than would be possible by simply raising one's voice. The loudspeaker carries the Word to the hearer as if he were standing directly before him who is proclaiming it. It makes possible the establishment of an intimacy between the speaker and the hearer which, in earlier times, was not possible for men meeting in great numbers or in a huge hall. Chant, on the contrary, has a stylizing effect on words that precludes this intimacy.

The pericope belongs to different literary forms. There are texts which, because they are couched in more solemn forms, immediately seem to demand the chant: the beatitudes, the prologue of St. John's Gospel, the hymn to charity (1 Cor. 13), or in general, all texts with the quality of hymns. Other texts seem predisposed against the chant, e.g., the disciplinary exhortations of St. Paul to his communities. The traditional chanting of the epistle and the Gospel in our liturgy makes no allowance for differences in literary genre. This is not apparent as long as these parts of the Mass are sung in a foreign language, but the listener will become aware of it when these texts are sung in his own language. Moreover, it would seem that the tradition of reading in the Latin liturgy stems not from the practice of proclaiming the Word, but rather from the educational device of committing material to memory, as today in many cultures sacred texts are still learned by rote, and, in order to do so, men sing them. By means of the chant a text was lifted out of the everyday experience of life and rendered more solemn.

For certain texts and for certain occasions today's hearer still finds this practice fitting, although for the rest he himself is not accustomed to singing in his own cultural milieu. This fact is characterized by the following: as the liturgical movement made progress in Germany, the Christmas Gospel, which originally was chanted, was solemnly proclaimed in German at midnight Mass. The people found this unadorned speech lacking in richness and derogatory to the solemnity of the feast. But if the Gospel were to be chanted in German every day, or every Sunday, then for most congregations this would not be so evident. The requirements differ from one community to the next and from one liturgical solemnity to the next. Hence, it is probable that customs will quickly be established.

Whether a Gospel procession takes place or not basically determines the choice between spoken and sung forms. Experience seems to show that after a solemn Gospel procession the chant no longer seems out of place; when it is not repugnant to the literary form of the text, the chant is a foregone conclusion: it is either taken for granted or immediately expected. If by reason of the Gospel procession the proclamation of the Good News becomes a solemn act, then chant rather than speech is in order. Where the Gospel is sung and the epistle is read, the Gospel is made to seem more noble and is emphasized in a special way.

Therefore, it would not be correct simply to chant all the lessons because hitherto divine worship has been sung in Latin. But neither would it be correct simply to read all the lessons because up to this time people have not been accustomed to singing in the vernacular. The difference between reading and singing the lessons is to be studied in individual cases, with consideration given to literary genre, to the day or the feast, to individual circumstances and the structure and the customs of the community. In general, the singing of the Gospel will have priority over the singing of the epistle. But the ability of those who have to do the reading/singing should be taken into account. An epistle well read is better than one ill-sung. Good reading is not a simple matter; and bad singing is better than bad reading.

The psalm of the "service of the Word" (the *Gradual*) should, properly speaking, always be sung. It belongs to the literary classification of song, and in the history of our liturgy it has always been so treated. Musical treatment is immediately connected today with the psalms and psalmody, while no other texts seem absolutely to require singing. In the case of the psalms, singing is not artificial but proper to their execution.

Sung or Spoken Orations

As in the case of the readings, certain requirements also surround the chanting of the official prayers. The readings are directed to the congregation, and for this reason they must reach the hearer in a way calculated to make the greatest possible impression. The official prayer, like a message and mandate from the whole liturgical assembly, is directed to God. Today, as in the past, there is an immediate necessity for the prayer to be more solemn than everyday speech and more objective than personal prayer. This is effected in the chant.

An utterance in *recto tono* forbids any variation if it is not to become a parody of the chant. But *recto tono* gets a bad mark as unsatisfactory chant just as a matter of principle, if the rhythm and the meaning of the words get an uneven recitation on one tone. The object of the chant is that the words will become empty shells, clear forms; *recto tono* aims at unobstructed communication.

In the official prayers there is no question—as there is in the readings—of literary genres which might be in opposition to the chant. For the readings the loudspeaker and the microphone are legitimate means of proclamation; the Word will reach the listener better when the voice is muted, because the loudspeaker will amplify it. For the prayers, the microphone and the loudspeaker present a more artistic expedient for acoustical purposes. To mute the voice and consciously use the loudspeaker as a means of amplifying it would be to make the petition a private prayer; indeed, it would be unsuitably cheap and sensational to produce a ringing sound through the loudspeaker as in a radio broadcast. The official prayer requires, where the possibility or the necessity of electrical amplification is present, that its reader should use to advantage his own physical ability and should raise his voice for the chant, so that all those in whose name the prayer is said can hear him. Only then has his prayer the character of an official and public petition for those who hear it through the loudspeaker.

The chant is a clear and appropriate sign for distinguishing the official prayer of the Church from all other prayers, and for marking it as the high point of the liturgy. It is an element of solemnity. Because the celebrant has not been permitted up to the present to offer the official prayer in the vernacular, the prayer has been neglected wherever people took pains with the liturgical chants or with the liturgy, but were unable to sing the high Mass in Latin. They were not able to begin singing in the liturgy precisely where they should have begun with it. All singing should begin with the chanting of the official prayers and in particular with the chanting of the solemn eucharistic prayer as the high point of the liturgical celebration.

Handling the Chant in Congregational Singing: the Psalms, the Pater Noster, the Credo

The chant is properly a soloist's performance. In particular instances where the community engages in the psalmody, elements of improvisation have been refined: the cadence comes at a fixed rhythmical point; the psalmody moves to a regular rhythm; the impression of a congregation singing is preeminently a rhythmical one, an impression of to-and-fro, up-and-down. Psalmody at the hands of a congregation is not a proclamation but a meditation. Gregorian music does not make any clear distinction between psalm tones for the cantor and for the choir's singing of the psalms.

Modern possibilities for musical performance give free rein to chant or singing by the congregation. However, this demands a superior choral group that will not let itself be influenced by the rhythm of the psalm-form, but will follow the lead of a director who controls the improvised elements in the psalmody. The singing of the lesson—which means also of the psalms in the "fore-Mass"—and most of the prayers, is not the function of such a choir.

The *Pater Noster* can now be spoken or sung by the celebrant alone or by the whole liturgical assembly. When sung or spoken jointly, the *Pater Noster* loses the character of a chant and takes on the character of an acclamation, since the congregation does not begin to sing abruptly; the celebrant introduces the prayer and the congregation concludes it. Fundamentally, this is the same form it has in the Mozarabic, where the celebrant used to recite the petition, and the acclamation of the community in the *Amen* gave a solemn assent to the petition. In melody the acclamations give proof of a different set of requirements from those of the chant or cantillation-form: a good and proper chant is not, unconditionally and at the same time, a good and correct way of making an acclamation. This is noticeable in the melodic preparation for the congregational singing of the *Pater Noster*.

The *Credo* appears first in the West as something to be sung because of its very nature; therefore, we may suppose, men saw this profession of faith as a solemn and formal utterance, and those living under the Franks translated this formula into song.[14] In the development of church music the *Credo* has taken on a very different function: in listening to a choir sing the *Credo* people were not so much performing an act of confession as being given an opportunity for meditation on the truths of faith. Certainly there is nothing wrong with that, but it is questionable whether that is the function which the *Credo* is meant to have in the liturgy of the Mass. In many places the celebrant does not wait for the end of the *Credo,* because it is sung during the presentation of the gifts brought to the priest—though this is characteristic of the history of our liturgy in the last hundred years. The singing which is itself a rite became either an accompaniment to the presentation (as in the case of the *Kyrie* and the *Sanctus*) or withered away, as in the case of the *Gradual.* Already the Gregorian melodies did not do justice to the *Credo* as an act of faith. They are definite musical compositions, songs, and they have assimilated the characteristics inherent in the performance of antiphonal psalmody. General experience of life shows us that an act of profession and/or obligation, for example, an oath, may be performed either when *all* speak the text or

[14] Cf. H. Hucke, "Die Gesänge des Messordinariums, Funktion und Gestalt," in *Musik und Altar,* 17 (1965), pp. 103ff. In French: "Le Credo, la fonction et la forme," in *Eglise qui chante,* 63-64 (1965), pp. 151ff.

when *one* person speaks the text; in either case, it is acclaimed item by item. This last form has been a distinctive mark of the *Credo,* especially where it is understood as a more solemn act of faith, most recently in the liturgy of the Easter Vigil. This example shows us that the *Credo* as an act of faith is not required, or at least is not on all occasions required to be sung in order to be solemn.

A lector or a reader or a performer working through a third party (for example, a choir) in successive alternation of texts in different choirs, or between the precentor and the congregation, but without the acclamation of all concerned, does not do justice to the form which the act of faith requires, and does not give any indication of what is meant. The usual form when there is question of an act of this kind is, in Western culture, speech; elsewhere it may assume any form that is possible or customary. In the West there are also simple and flexible forms for singing the *recitative* which perhaps should not be excluded. The *Credo* sung by the community or by alternating choirs in Gregorian chant, or chanted to some similar music in the vernacular is, however, really not the performance of a confessional act, but singing *about* the faith. Such singing has its place on pilgrimages or in St. Peter's Square. And it has the same place in life as the singing of a (confessional) hymn. But whether such singing as this is what was meant to be a profession of faith *in* the Mass, or whether the *Credo* in the Mass should stand as an act of faith, is a matter for the rubrics to settle.

Exclamations and Acclamations

When a man calls out, he expects an answer, or at least an echo. The acclamation is an answer, even when it has not been preceded by an acoustically perceptible summons.

One who is silent in the face of a challenge and yet is physically in a position to give an answer to it, shows either lack of regard or lack of interest: in such a case, the silence does not mean nothing, but it says that the one who should give an answer has no relation to the summons. The answer to a summons and an acclamation cannot be delegated to another unless, again, to so respond is physically impossible. No one can commission a colleague in his stead to answer a summons issued by a superior: this would be to fail with regard to the summons and to lack respect for the one who issues it. He who is silent in the presence of a clamorous multitude, puts himself at a distance from the clamor and from the multitude. The form and circumstance of the acclamation can suggest that the execution is partially entrusted to a delegate, but then this partial execution must be done by acclamation.

If I call out and the one I call upon comes nearer to me, then my cry changes involuntarily into speech. The summons and the acclamation as such can be either sung or spoken. They, too, are not autonomous musical forms or even forms to compose for: singing is a way of performing a summons or an acclamation. By common and unanimous consent, they both require a real *una voce,* unison treatment, to be considered singing.

The suitable form of the answer depends on the content of the summons. In the direct dialogue of summons and response, musical elaboration would be out of place; it would be affected and would distract from the real content of the answer. Whoever creates a musical composition out of *yes,* no longer answers with *yes,* but with music. But it can be that the summons requires more than a simple *yes,* that a simple *yes* would not be enough. Where acclamation becomes an inspiration, it urges every fiber of the body into expression: people clap; they make physical gestures; they dance; they send up their shouts with every means at their disposal. Even in the West not only children do this. The most solemn and the highest form of acclamation is, therefore, to be absolutely "lost"—immersed—in the singing.

The Liturgical Summons and Acclamation

In the liturgy there are both summonses and acclamations, namely, chants (cantillations) and acclamations, respectively, in the form of dialogues between the ministers and the whole liturgical assembly. The liturgy authorizes only the leader and his deputy to address the assembly, and the communal character of the answer is the expression of the community of the assembly.

Where in the liturgy a summons or challenge is issued, it is always intended for the entire assembly. These are the moments of invitation to prayer, at the proclamation of the Gospel, when the body of the Lord is held up: "Ecce Agnus Dei", at the dismissal, and when, in the litany, the desires of the community are being formulated. The experience of daily life should teach us that the acclamations in the liturgy must be carried out by everyone. The *Amen* and the *Deo Gratias,* the *Et cum spiritu tuo, Habemus ad Dominum, Te rogamus, audi nos,* or *Miserere nobis,* no man can delegate to a choir or to a cleric; he cannot even delegate them to his neighbor: he must himself sing or say them, otherwise his own consent will be lacking, otherwise the *whole* liturgical assembly will not be making the acclamation. And when the *Pater Noster* is not sung as an acclamation by the entire community, but is chanted by the celebrant in the name of the community as its official prayer, it is still essentially the acclamation of the community to the chant of the celebrant; this is as important as the signature to a document drawn up in his own name by an official person.

Again, in the liturgy a summons or an acclamation can be either sung or spoken. But the liturgical summons or challenge is already an invitation to leave everyday matters behind. Hence, the summons used in the liturgy should be raised above daily forms of speech to the solemnity of singing. Singing is the most significant factor in solemnizing the liturgical summons. The summons of the liturgical representative and the acclamation or response of the assembly are not dialogues between individual persons; hence they must be objectified by singing. The acclamation in the liturgy is always a communal and solemn act; hence, it has its own proper singing form.

The summons and the acclamation in the liturgy are most often joined in the assembly. If the petition is sung, then it requires as a rule that the summons—the invitation to prayer—and the acclamation be sung, too.

In worship the musical form of the acclamation must correspond to its content. If the *Amen* of the oration were made a musical piece, then this would not be a "decorated" *Amen* but an "ersatz" *Amen:* it would have become something other, by means of music. When someone is moved to a *jubilus* on the *Sursum corda,* then it performs another function. To the words of the *Pater Noster* taught us by the Lord himself, we can add nothing in the way of musical ornament. It is appropriate that we should give these words a solemn form where they are said in the liturgy and occur as a solemn rite; that we should, as it were, clothe our voices in festal garments by reciting the words in song. If that singing were only music, then we should have disguised the words.

In the same way, the *Sanctus* requires us to stay within a ritualistic word-formula, and demands that the acclamation-type of music not be supplanted by any other kind of musical composition. The *Sanctus* is not, therefore, an autonomous musical form. But the acclamation of the *Sanctus* allows, even demands, that we employ whatever we have in the line of musical talents or other means at our disposal, because the *Sanctus* is a song of praise, a song of praise of his majesty. This hymn would be a paltry one if it were to be confined to the words. It is extremely significant that when we sing the acclamation of the angels we do not do so in speech. For how should we speak and not sing when we raise our voices in the cry of "the heavens and the heavenly powers and of the blessed Seraphim", and with "angels and archangels, thrones and dominations, and all the heavenly hosts" together proclaim his majesty? With the *Sanctus* all congregational singing must begin. Where there is a choir in the congregation, they should lead the congregation in the *Sanctus.* It is through their art, perhaps through the concerted accompaniment of the congregational singing, that a more noble and a more solemn type of singing will take shape. And so, too, we should permit inanimate creation, wherever it has a voice, the organ, the other musical instruments, to join in the *Sanctus.* The *Sanctus* is the place "to praise (the Lord) with sound of trumpet,/praise him with lute and harp./Praise him with timbrel and dance,/ praise him with strings and pipes./O praise him with resounding cymbals,/. . . Let everything that lives and breathes/give praise to the Lord".[15]

But the choir cannot be a substitute for the singing of the entire congregation, any more than it can substitute for the celebrant's singing at high mass. The congregation and everyone in the congregation must sing together, for the *Sanctus* is an acclamation of the most solemn kind. It may be that the choir by itself can sing the *Sanctus* more artistically than when the whole congregation sings it. The *Sanctus* is not a musical composition but a rite, a liturgical act, which the whole congregation and everyone in the congregation has to perform. We are speaking here not of the *active participation* of the community in the *Sanctus,* but of the *active participation* of the community in the liturgical solemnity through the *Sanctus.* Where a choir substitutes for the community in singing the *Sanctus,* singing, as an act of ritual and as an immensely important cultic sign, is called in question.

Singing and Music

To sing a popular song and to speak it are two different things. When we speak the text of a song, a cantata, a motet, then we are no longer considering the song, the cantata, the motet, and this is not a substitution: speaking the text of a song does not correspond to what is meant by the term *song.* Where there is question not of chant, summons, and acclamation, but of a song properly so-called, speaking is no alternative to singing. The spoken song is a song no more; it is a poem.

Where a hymn is spoken, another form comes into being. Only on the premises that the text is poetical and is recognized as a poetical form does the sung form find an equivalent in the spoken form: a hymn which is spoken remains a hymn, and a psalm which is recited remains a psalm. But where the text is not poetical and is not recognized as a poetical form, the text of the song which is spoken returns to whatever literary form it

[15] Psalm 150.

originally had. The spoken text of a song becomes either a poem, or a tale, or an aphorism, or some other type. In any case, it is not a song.

When men sing, the voice is louder and more penetrating than when they speak; and in singing more than the rational content of the words is given voice. Singing is a different expression of life from speech; it is more compelling than speech. Singing is a giving-away of the self: the man who sings gives up his own individual speaking voice in favor of an objective sound which the listener recognizes and applies to himself. St. Augustine describes how: "I am well aware that the holy or sacred words when they are sung, plunge my soul into more joyful and more ardent fervor of devotion than when they are not sung; while every movement of our soul has some deep and hidden relationship according to its own nature with songs and voices according to their nature, which excite and move us." [16]

Singing shapes a community. And this is not simply some remote theory or idealistic talk: men may experience this in their daily lives. When a group of men come together they can, no doubt, speak of different things in different ways, but they cannot sing different things and do different things while they sing. They can speak as a group, but to do so implies at least that they have a particular occasion and a particular text. To sing together hardly needs a particular occasion or any particular text. It can be that all men may hear the one man who is speaking. But then they do so only because of what he is saying or because it is he who is saying it. But if he sings, then they listen to him because he is singing, whoever he may be; and it may be that each one who is listening long ago heard and recognizes what he is singing. Singing and singing together require involvement. I must do more than when I merely speak, especially since, in daily life, I am no longer accustomed to sing. When I sing I pledge myself in a more than everyday fashion. Every revolutionary movement enlists the service of song. What distinguishes those who sing from those who do not sing together is the ac-

---

[16] St. Augustine, *Confessions,* X, 33.

knowledgment of the physical or artistic inability to sing, or a willed decision not to participate, or the distraction of some other matter, or the detachment of someone who wishes to listen.

The alternative to song is speech. Where a man cannot sing a song, let him be silent and not speak it. Or, in the place of the song, let there be music and people can listen to it: where it is question of a song properly so-called and not of an acclamation, then listening can be an alternative to singing and in its place there can be music or instrumental renditions.

Music and song are essential elements of a feast day. The bridal couple, who have not been concerned with music in worship throughout their lives, may still, nonetheless, have music at their wedding. Even solemn occasions of a worldly nature— solemnities on the national and/or corporate, community level —require music, the so-called "musical setting". But it is not merely a "musical setting", since it represents an elementary human need for a solemn occasion. Every nation has its national anthem.

People take part in the chant while they listen to it, whereas people take part in the acclamation while they acclaim. In song and music man can take part either while singing or while listening. Singing can be either in unison or in dialogue with others. Communal or congregational singing binds people together: it acts like a circle eliminating cliques and disparateness, bridging differences. The articulation of a congregation in different groups, each with distinctive functions, is removed through communal singing of all the groups in a beautiful common refrain. The alternation of parts in singing brings a congregation together like so many limbs in a single body and is an expression and sign of the correspondence of the members with one another. Therefore, the singing for a procession is done in alternating parts.

Listening to Music

Today in the West it happens that men listen to music at an earlier age than they sing or play a musical instrument themselves. Where music is considered an art, sharing in it, as a rule,

means to do so as a listener, for only if I am an artist, can I myself perform this art. The works of the plastic arts and of architecture are created once and for all. On the other hand and in
opposition to this, the art of music is never finished; what has
been created once must be reproduced anew on each occasion;
the re-production or re-presentation must in its turn also be art.
Music performed by one who is not an artist is not true art but
a surrogate for art. He who performs a musical work is not an
artist because of this performance; only by reason of his own
artistic execution is he an artist; but he is so not of necessity, and
he is not absolutely or unconditionally a good advocate for the
art of music.

At the present moment some well-defined groups may be observed in the process of adapting or modifying the Church's
liturgy by means of music. But this is the exception, and it is no
longer a question of social groups, but rather of groups at different levels of musical appreciation (perhaps of amateurs or
culture-hounds), or of music fans. By the growth of public con-
certs, and especially through modern communications media—
radio, TV, and recordings—the social unity of music listeners
has been greatly weakened. Therefore, as the ways and means of
receiving music are multiplied, the range of those receiving it
grows wider than ever. For the liturgical solemnity this is more
true than it is in any concert hall, since the liturgical assembly,
as a rule, will not consist of a musical public: the listener does
not come—or at least he should not come—to church to listen
to music. On the other hand, to be sure, this means that he has
fewer musical prejudices. Apart from this, music in the liturgical
solemnity is not music absolutely, and the stylistic canons of the
tradition of music in the churches have given rise to certain customs or listening habits which have, in fact, taken hold of the
very essence of church music.[17]

Yet, it cannot be denied that the music being offered for liturgical services today poses a problem of the most serious kind, and

[17] The problem of listening to the music, and of the listener in the liturgy
is still waiting for a thorough investigation.

not only with regard to a new consciousness of the liturgy and the liturgical reform. And modern communications media have set up even in the remotest hamlets a wholly new standard of comparison. Fifty years ago the choir or organist might at the most serve as artistic measuring-rod for the neighboring church. Today the listener brings the standard of measurement from the TV set in his own home.

Singing in the Liturgy

As an element of intensification as well as for establishing unanimity and providing solemnity, the singing of the solemn liturgy plays a necessary, integral, and stable role.[18] Liturgical singing can be the accompaniment of a rite: in escorting the ministers, in the *Introit, Offertory,* and *Communion* processions of the Mass. But liturgical singing can also be a rite in itself: in the hymn (so long as this does not accompany a rite), and in the *Gloria* of the Mass.

Singing the liturgy is the concern of the community. Where the ministers sing it, it is not so much a question of singing in its true sense, but of a summons or a chant; or they sing with the congregation as part of the community. When the choir sings, it does so representing the whole congregation rather than as a group within the community.

Accordingly, speech in the liturgy is not another expression of the singing. A spoken *Introit* is no longer a sung entrance-song; it takes on the character of a *lectio brevis,* or of a prayer, or of a speech, or still another character: speech in particular cannot be seen in any other guise; it can be murmured or declaimed singly or by several alternating. The text forms of the singing accompaniments are not composed to be spoken but to be sung; and this the creative power of the singer must execute. Neither the one who speaks them nor those who hear them spoken will derive spiritual profit from them, because in the course of the liturgical function the time for meditation—which is provided in the act of singing—is now lacking. Thus, they have become

[18] *Constitution on the Sacred Liturgy,* Art. 112.

disconnected quotations without the least function, so many false signs by which the movement of the liturgical action is simply interrupted and its structure obscured.

Only where a poetical form remains perceptible will the speaking of a text, instead of its singing, acquire a new form. The spoken hymn remains a hymn, and the spoken psalm remains psalmody. But it is not the same whether a community sings a hymn or a psalm or whether they speak them. Where they speak them, they constitute a speech chorus: the melodic component shrinks and the rhythmical is emphasized; the speech chorus charms us first of all by its rhythm. That it is easier to speak in a speech chorus than to sing in unison is not so: choral speech is an art form that requires considerable skill for mastery. In our liturgy, choral speech has, up to this time, been used only as a second-best solution for the dearth of singers. The artistic possibilities, but also the requirements and the limitations of choral speech in the theater should be studied.

The most popular form of singing, even far and away the most popular form of singing as a whole, is the *lied* (song). The German language especially possesses in its hymns a treasure of ecclesiastical music in the mother tongue that is worthy to stand beside its store of Latin hymns. In the Roman liturgy handed down to us, the song-form (*lied*) plays a very small role in comparison with its role in the Eastern liturgies. And the efforts to bring about a "liturgical *rapprochement*" of this form and the singing of the liturgical texts in the vernacular in many places has raised questions about the song-form and the traditional hymn, since the song-form requires a poetical text and the liturgical text of the Roman liturgy will allow only a transference into the song-form by way of paraphrase. The singing required by the liturgy can never be satisfied with the song-form; it cannot dispense with the psalms, and it would weaken the acclamations to turn them into songs. But neither will sung liturgy in the vernacular be able to get along without the most popular form of community singing, and where there are no hymns (*lied*), they must be created. For if the people are invited to sing, we ought not to prescribe theoretical forms for them. That people should be allowed to sing in their own forms is hardly less important than that they should be allowed to sing in their own language. The place of church "songs" in the liturgy will be where song has its own rightful place.[19]

Song as the Accompaniment of a Rite

By song as the accompaniment of a rite is not meant definite music or definite texts, but that there should be singing. Singing accompaniment to the liturgy should not merely occupy the congregation for the duration of the ceremony or cover up the restlessness occurring while the ceremony is in progress; rather, it should engage the whole congregation in the ceremony, unlock the spiritual rite for them and endow it with greater solemnity.

The sung accompaniments of the Mass liturgy are, as such, processionals. History and general experience show that a special kind of performance is especially suited to the processional, namely, the alternation of *schola* or precentors singing with the whole assembly. The processional must, in addition, be sung in alternation and not *in directum*. For the processional is not a means of gathering the assembly together, but a manifestation of that assembled unity. And the musical form corresponding to it is not a closed, but an open form, a form that does not put a constraint upon the expanding assembly, but produces harmony among its members and groups. To processional singing belongs, therefore, the singing of groups or cantors or precentors. The singing of such a group can be very simple; it can, for example, be stanzas of a song, or refrains alternating with the singing of the whole assembly. But there are many opportunities to introduce other artistic effects by the use of part-songs and musical instruments.

The music of the entrance song allows for the richest musical adornment.[20] By its festive character it expresses the solemnity

---

[19] Cf. B. Huijbers, "Wert und Grenzen des Liedes in der Liturgie," in preparation. Cf. *supra,* footnote 7.

[20] J. Gelineau, "La psalmodie et les chants processionaux," in preparation. Cf. *supra,* footnote 7.

of the ensuing celebration. The singing of the *Communion* verse requires discretion in execution; an overly rich musical form would detract from, rather than emphasize, what is taking place. In singing the *Introit,* it is absolutely necessary that the whole congregation join in the action, since, to be sure, the communal singing represents the assembly's part in the entrance procession and unites the assembly in one mind for the following liturgical solemnity. Singing the *Communion* verse expresses participation in the singing and the communal fellowship of the sacred banquet. The form in which the whole community participates in the music is in the singing of the *Communion* song, which is set within narrower limits than the entrance song; nothing else would be suitable if all are to take part in the song while moving up to Communion. Where there is no procession for bringing up the gifts, there is no occasion for singing a procession hymn. In this case the congregation may sing some kind of composition (*lied*) in unison, or singing by the choir or an organ interlude may lead the assembly to meditation and direct their attention to the secret prayers which give expression to the communal character of the ceremony.

The renewal in the liturgy of singing accompaniment cannot originate in the texts of the Roman Missal. These texts received their form from Gregorian Chant. They owe their present form to their original purpose of being presented by a choir, and from the fact that they were set to music by means which the Roman *scholae cantorum* employed in their day. The requirements of these forms do not permit a parish to make adaptations of the texts unaided, since the antiphon-texts are too numerous and too little practicable for singing by a congregation. Most of these texts do not do justice to their function, namely, to bring close to the community the rites they accompany. Today we can often succeed better with other texts and other music.

The alternative to singing is not speaking—but silence or music. Where it is not possible to sing, organ playing can be substituted. At the same time, organ playing does not have all the effectiveness that singing has.

Singing as Rite: the Gloria

Where singing is a rite, the rite itself becomes singing and is raised above itself to become more than mere words. Then we are no longer dealing with a mere text. In the text of a hymn a man is only speaking, but when a man is carrying out a rite, he is not acting in an ordinary way, but is doing something quite different. As singing is not a necessary element in every liturgical action but is an integral part of the solemn liturgical action, so, too, not every liturgical act demands that rites be sung: the *Gloria* is not a necessary part of every Mass. The rite of the *Gloria* would only properly be prescribed if it were to be correctly performed, that is, if it can be sung.

In the words of this hymn the People of God has sung his holiness through the centuries. In the *Sanctus* we join in the angels' chorus, and in this hymn we give voice to the whole of creation. The hymn is our song, and in the *Gloria* our own song has become part of the Mass liturgy. In the Gloria-form the singing of the redeemed People of God has found a classical form. Yet it may be asked whether it would not correspond to the meaning of the rite and the peculiar nature of the hymn if we were to give new life to this song of praise, too, by using our own words, in the Mass, in a song-form of our own day.

In form the *Gloria* is an early Christian "prose-hymn". In many places this form poses problems of adaptation. It does not correspond to the form which folk and communal hymns have in most cultures. Hence the *Gloria* does not chime with a wide experience of hymn-singing, but, in many places, awakens associations with other forms and is thought of as something other. In the West, most informed persons will involuntarily connect the *Gloria* with certain forms of subjective lyricism which have a similar structure, and by this fact the *Gloria* is emptied of meaning. Characteristically there is no other musical text in the liturgy so widely used for speech choruses as the *Gloria*. Moreover, the comprehension or understanding of the *Gloria* is thereby considerably impaired—even as the *Credo* has been—under the influence of antiphonal psalmody and the adoption of the "alternate-side" performance when it is sung. So it becomes pseudo-psalmody, in the performance of which the structure of the text together with its content is obscured.

However it is presented, the performance should be such as to make the structure of the *Gloria* clearer; only then will the musical form have done justice to the text. At the same time, care must be taken that compositions for the *Gloria* correspond to the scope of the hymn-experience of the community so that the *Gloria* will be recognized as a hymn.

It is suitable to the *Gloria* that the community have at its disposal every kind of musical arrangement that choir, organ and instruments afford. In contradistinction to the *Sanctus*-acclamation, the singing of the *Gloria* can be delegated; it can be handed over to the choir: the acclamation a man must perform for himself in his own person; with singing, a man can delegate it to another if by so doing it can be performed more beautifully and more fittingly. Whether the *Gloria* should be sung by the whole congregation, or in alternating manner by the choir and the congregation, or by the choir alone, is to be decided according to conditions and circumstances.

Singing and the Structure of the Liturgical Solemnity

Every public solemnity or feast has a form and structure; ready at hand are certain musical possibilities as means for articulating and giving coherence to that form. People do not first have nothing but music and then have nothing but speeches; in the same way, people do not allow uniform and homogeneous musical compositions to succeed one another uninterruptedly.

The sung and singable parts of the Mass have been understood since the later Middle Ages (insofar as they were not to be sung by the higher ministers—priest, deacon, subdeacon—but by the cantor, the choir or the people) to comprise the *Ordinary* and the *Proper of the Mass*.[21] For this we follow, after all, the practical, external criteria: the parts of the Mass that remain the

---

[21] More characteristically, the *Credo* has kept an exceptional position in the liturgical hymnals up to this time.

same are found in the *Ordinary,* and those that change from feast to feast in the *Proper.* As a result, the *Proper* and especially the *Ordinary of the Mass* were grouped in musical cycles. In the liturgical celebrations either both cycles (*Proper* and *Ordinary*) were dovetailed with one another, or people limited themselves more or less to one cycle for musical presentation, the *Ordinary of the Mass,* which became, musically, "the Mass".

The reform in liturgy and church music cannot start from this classification according to *Ordinary* and *Proper;*[22] rather, we must now inquire after the nature and kind of each one of these parts. Within the different parts, under chant (cantillation), summons, acclamation, and singing, a further distinction must be made according to the function each fulfills.

Singing and the different singable parts of the Mass are at one and the same time structural elements of the liturgy that have a function also with regard to the whole of the structure of the liturgical solemnity. When the musician does not pay attention to the forms and kinds of singing in the liturgy, and the function that singing/music has to fulfill in it—if, for example, acclamation and singing are treated as nothing more than the stanzas of a true song or hymn—then the structure of the liturgical celebration is at the same time blurred. But also, where the differences of kinds and sorts of singing/music in the liturgy are observed, the result can be an assimilation of the different sung and singable parts of the liturgy. When, for example, acclamation and singing are handled without distinction in the same form of alternate-side renditions and in similar musical settings, then the whole liturgical celebration will gradually and inevitably be absorbed into a new and monotonous antiphonal song-type performance. Such monotony is not only an esthetic and musical problem; it is a liturgical problem, since in it the very construct of the liturgical action becomes, of necessity, meaningless.

[22] The first to work this out is probably J. Gelineau in his book *Chant et Musique dans le Culte Chrétien* (Paris, 1962). German edition: *Die Musik im christlichen Gottesdienst* (Regensburg, 1965). Different language editions could be cited which I am unable to identify in particular.

It is the task of the church musician, through every means at his disposal—melody, rhythm, form, execution, by the concerted action of different types: the organ, musical instruments and their different uses—to set off acclamation and singing at liturgical solemnities according to their functions, and so to make the structure of the liturgical solemnity more emphatic. The question must not be whether the choir should sing the *Proper,* or whether or not it should sing Palestrina, or whether the choir should cooperate in the processional by singing four-part compositions with instrumental accompaniment. We must ask in what way, and with which musical means at our disposal, we can contribute to the liturgical function in a meaningful way so that the proclamation of the Gospel will be the high point of the service of the Word, while the hymns guide us to that goal in a suitable fashion. And how can we make the eucharistic prayer the climax of the sacrifice, the *Sanctus* the climax of the singing, and through their solemnity enhance the solemnity of the whole eucharistic sacrifice?

Conclusion

The fundamental problem of church music in the liturgical reform is sometimes seen to consist in permitting the people to sing and in having the liturgical texts sung in the vernacular. In contrast to this position, it may be held that it is the task of church music to safeguard the heritage of church music that has come down to us from the past, as well as to keep watch over the artistic character of church music, choral singing, and the Latin language; that spokesmen for church music belong to the most determined enemies of the vernacular in the liturgy is well known.

Where the tasks of church music are envisaged in this fashion, the church music "Establishment" is held to *be* church music and church musical art. But our church music has lost its character as a sign. Its liturgical function is confused with another function—to adjust the liturgy of the Church to the changes in contemporary taste and social structure. Today singing in the Church has become a decoration for the ceremonies, a little display of musical treasures, an alternative to speaking a given liturgical text and to singing in the church. It is, therefore, not the liturgical movement and the liturgical reform which have, in fact, raised questions about traditional church music and its artistic validity. On the contrary, church music is using the liturgical reform to liberate itself from its undignified position, from this blind alley into which it has strayed, so as to find its way back again to true art.

The liturgist is accustomed to see the task of church music as primarily the composition for prescribed texts and the avoidance of abuses; in more recent times, the demand for the right apportionment of roles, especially with respect to the people, has claimed attention. But such fussy concern for rubrics does not do justice to the singing in the liturgy and to the meaning of singing as a liturgical sign. The liturgist, even as the church musician himself, must understand the singing once more as a liturgical sign rather than a performance, one which is more meaningful and more significant than most other liturgical actions. And they must learn anew the speech gestures of singing, because "even inanimate instruments, like the flute or the harp, may produce sound, but if there is no difference in the notes, how shall it be known what is piped or harped? If the trumpet give forth an uncertain sound, who will prepare for battle?" [23]

[23] 1 Cor. 14, 7-8.

✠ Hugo Aufderbeck/*Erfurt, W. Germany*

The Liturgical Assembly in the Diaspora

Christians in the diaspora are like stones which lie outdoors in wind and weather; they grow weather-beaten. Experience shows that throughout the diaspora the individual Christian and the isolated Christian family have not been able to hold out for long if they have not come together as an assembly. The eight-day period seems to be the length of time in which a man can be left to his own strength. But then the scattered ones must come together or they will lose sight of their brothers and their Lord. The Sunday convocation is, therefore, the crucial point of support for the Christ-life of the community in the diaspora. As was said of the first Christians, so it must be said of the Christians in the diaspora: they were gathered together (Acts 4, 31; 12, 12; 14, 27; 15, 30).[1]

A gathering of the Catholics of the diaspora in some outpost as a rule makes little impression. "There are not many wise according to the flesh, not many mighty, not many noble" (1 Cor. 1, 26). No, what seems to the world foolish, what seems to

[1] Cf. J. Hofinger, J. Kellner, "Der priesterlose Gemeindegottesdienst in den Missionen," a series of articles in *Neue Zeitschrift für Missionwissenschaft* 14 (1956); *idem, Liturgische Erneuerung in der Weltmission* (Innsbruck, 1957), pp. 204-63; J. Hofinger, *Mission und Liturgie* (Mainz, 1960), pp. 118-22; H. Aufderbeck, "Stationsgottesdienst," in *Liturgisches Jahrbuch* 14 (Münster, 1964), pp. 172-84; H. Theissing, H. Aufderbeck, *Ich bin bei Euch* (Leipzig, 1954).

it weak, what it regards as lowborn and of no account, indeed, what is naught (cf. 1 Cor. 1, 27-28), is to be found gathered together in some little room. And yet there lies within this assembly a hidden splendor. For all who are here gathered together are "God's chosen ones, holy and beloved" (Col. 3, 12). In this assembly there co-exist, insofar as the number, appearance, and age of those gathered together are concerned, all that is outwardly pitiable and a hidden majesty that stems from their calling and their grace. It is in very truth a "miserable" assembly, and, in its misery, a blessed assembly.

By reason of a threefold power this assembly becomes life, joy and enthusiasm. The first of these powers, the one that brings the scattered members together, is love for the brethren who are of one mind with one another. The Christians of the diaspora, who in their day-to-day environment will often abandon their belief and experience loneliness, and will be regarded by others with misgivings and uneasiness, will experience their *koinonia* (Acts 2, 42). This is the expression of their "brotherhood" (1 Pet. 2, 17). In the assembly it is granted to them to experience how all "love one another with fraternal charity" (Rom. 12, 10). For if they only come together to see one another, to converse with one another, and to have a cup of coffee together, this meeting, too, is not without its reward. It is, indeed, not a liturgical assembly, but an *agape,* from which a great and mighty power springs.

The second power which brings scattered Christians together is faith in the Lord. Because they adore him, they want to have him in their midst; they want to listen to him and to pray in his name. For those who come together in the name of the Lord, he is there in their midst (Matt. 18, 20). *In medio ecclesiae:* in the midst of the assembly he opened his mouth. "He is present in his Word since it is he himself who speaks when the sacred Scriptures are read in the church. He is present, lastly, when the church prays and sings" (*Constitution on the Sacred Liturgy,* Art. 7).

The third force that brings together the Catholics of the diaspora is their care for one another: for the lukewarm, the indifferent, the fallen away, the unbelieving; for the children and the aged; for the sick, the suffering and the dying; for all who stand in need of God's help. This little assembly exists not only for itself, but "for many". A part of the service that it renders is "that supplications, prayers, intercessions and thanksgivings be made for all men. . . . For this is good and agreeable in the sight of God our Savior, who wishes all men to be saved and to come to the knowledge of the truth" (1 Tim. 2, 1-4). Their prayer is full of power, for "if two of you shall agree on earth about anything at all for which they ask, it shall be done for them by my Father in heaven" (Matt. 18, 19).

What form should the liturgical assembly have? After many experiments, the following form for an assembly without a priest is proposed:

The liturgical assembly begins, after a short introduction (words of greeting or welcome, a hymn, an announcement), with a reading from the Bible. A rather long passage from the Scriptures which is sufficiently unified, e.g., Luke 15; Matthew 24, 29—25, 13; 1 Corinthians 15, is read in three parts by the lector, each part introduced by a short introduction and ending with a meditative prayer, psalm, or hymn. A homily, which as a rule is read, explains the Word of Scripture. The congregation then prays the Apostles' Creed. The Scripture reading follows as the second part of "the people's prayer". Here we must pay attention to the order followed by the primitive Church: praise, thanksgiving, petition, atonement, praise. The prayers chosen may be those that belong to the fundamental prayer of the Church, so that in this way the Church's treasury of prayer may remain alive in the hearts of the faithful. The prayer must be so chosen that it will form a single whole with the reading from Scripture. The intercession, which is a firmly fixed element in the prayer of the community, makes the mission of the tiny congregation meaningful, since it is for the salvation of all men.

Then follows the third part, which allows the little flock to experience the fact that it is part "of the holy fellowship" with the entire flock and its shepherd, with the "family" of the diocese and their bishop, with the Catholic Church of the whole world and her ruler, even with all the "Saints" in heaven and on earth, whom the Lord has brought together from the four corners of the globe. In this part there is place, too, for the brethren to ask pardon of, and to forgive, one another from the heart, and for the collection of alms as a token that they will assist each other.

The blessing-prayer, the announcement of the coming feasts, and the Angelical Salutation close the assembly. It is important that this liturgical assembly be kept simple and clear in structure, plain and unadorned, homely and inviting in style.

The liturgical assembly in the diaspora will be correctly carried out only if certain definite conditions are fulfilled. It must be conducted by a lector who has been commissioned by the bishop or the pastor. The Constitution on the Sacred Liturgy expressly commands this. No one without a commission may assemble the community and proclaim the Word of God. It is by reason of this power delegated by the bishop that this assembly differs from the gatherings of the sects. The office of lector can be delegated only to one who has the charisma to perform the service. Essential to it are: the will to serve; the ability to read correctly the Word of God; the mental and spiritual powers of one "who might gather together into one the children of God who were scattered abroad" (John 11, 52); a kind and winning manner that will facilitate for the community a benevolent reception for the person and the acceptance of the Word of God.

We believe that the Holy Spirit is making men and women ready to undertake this service, for in every age he permits the growth within the community of the charism that he brings to it. One crucial prerequisite for the success of this liturgical assembly without a priest is that the manifold objections which are being brought against it be taken up and refuted by theologians. Many think and maintain that the simple "Bible Service" has something sectarian about it, that the distinction between priest and layman is being wiped out. Some pose the question of the efficacy of such an assembly in which no sacramental action takes place; others hold that no one is obliged thereto by the Church's law. The Constitution on the Sacred Liturgy brushes aside all these and other objections: "Bible services should be encouraged . . . on Sundays and feast days . . . particularly when no priest is available" (Art. 35, iv).

The regular Sunday liturgical assembly is of the greatest significance for the life of the believer in the diaspora, for it vanquishes the might of Satan. St. Ignatius of Antioch writes: "If you gather together frequently, the power of Satan is undone, and his deathly influence over your faith is broken" (Smyrn. 13, 1).

Moreover, the strengthening and increase of the faithful are effected. What is true of water in the sea holds good for believers in the diaspora. If water lies stagnant, it grows foul and malodorous. The community stays "sound in faith" (Tit. 1, 13; 2, 2) only if it is increasingly and constantly being moved by the Word of God. Otherwise it is "bewitched" (Gal. 3, 1), and in the environment of the diaspora it will fall immediately into fables, false ideologies and every possible kind of windy teaching (2 Tim. 4, 4; Eph. 4, 14).

Through the assembly the "brotherhood" of 1 Pet. 2, 47 becomes a fact of ever-widening importance. "He who comes not to the assembly, is already possessed by pride and has already judged himself" (Smyrn. 3, 3). He has placed himself outside the fellowship. But where, in spite of shortcomings and awkwardnesses, the assembly is held in honor, is sought out and loved, it becomes for the environment a consoling indication of brotherly love. "If . . . there should come in an unbeliever or an uninstructed person (to the assembly) . . . falling on his face, he will worship God, declaring that God is truly among you" (1 Cor. 14, 24). It is through the assembly that the brotherhood becomes manifest, and in the daily living out of our brotherliness that those outside our circle will be won over. Since all of

God's works are accomplished in a place and in a time, the faithful should in all places and at all times gather together, so that everywhere they may sing the praise of God, and everywhere prayer and petition may rise up to God for our salvation and for the salvation of the world.

PART II
BIBLIOGRAPHICAL
SURVEY

Thomas Vismans, O.P./*Nijmegen, Netherlands*

Liturgy or Rubrics?

Some Reactions to the Constitution on the Sacred Liturgy and the Instruction

In the Spanish periodical *Phase,* the Rev. P. Tena concludes his article, "A New Liturgy or New Rubrics?", with the following remarks: "The impact created by the Instruction issued by the Consilium and the expectation of March 7 (the date on which the new regulations were to be applied) have been considerably greater among the clergy and even the faithful than the impact created by the conciliar Constitution itself. Yet, it is impossible to understand the Instruction without the Constitution, and one cannot say that preparatory information about the latter has been lacking. Nevertheless, this comparison provokes the question: Have we really overcome the rubric mentality?" [1]

Doubtlessly the situation has varied from one country to another and the remarks of the author about the difference in reception given to the Constitution and to the Instruction apply to the situation in Spain and other countries where the liturgical movement has not as yet made much impression on the local attitudes. Other countries, particularly in Western Europe, received the Constitution enthusiastically because it was a monu-

[1] P. Tena, "Liturgia nueva o rúbricas nuevas?" in *Phase* 5 (1965), p. 9.

mental expression of views that had already been widely accepted, and because it opened the door to a renewal of the liturgy which appeared to many not only as desirable but necessary. There, one might almost say, the Constitution came just in time, and the Instruction a year too late.

The different situation in various countries, or regions, or even dioceses, is a plain fact that is easy to observe when one peruses the various liturgical periodicals or the reports of episcopal conferences published in the *Notitiae* of the Consilium.[2] It is also a fact that must be understood and taken into account. One has to regard as reasonable the request of certain bishops, no doubt because of the pastoral situation in their own dioceses, that no further innovations be introduced for the time being in, for example, the *Ordo Missae*. We must nevertheless hope that these particular situations will not be taken as the norm for the whole Church. At the same time, it would be a dangerous illusion to expect the renewal to take place all over the world at the same pace. This might create undesirable and harmful tensions, and would conflict with the basic idea of article 38 of the Constitution.

To return to Fr. Tena's question, we have to armit that, although the reaction to the Constitution was stronger in many countries than in Spain, in a certain sense the Instruction (or, more precisely, the actual introduction of some concrete changes prescribed by the Instruction) has had a far greater impact than the Constitution. It is only here that the inner dynamics of the Constitution became obvious, as did the effects, not only in extent but also in depth. The Instruction had the effect of a stone dropped into a stagnant pool, the waves of which extend to the very shore. Everyone who went to church was now almost bodily confronted with the renewal of the liturgy, and every priest in pastoral practice saw himself compelled not only to apply these innovations then and there—which automatically provoked in-

---

[2] "Consilium" is the post-conciliar commission, established in Rome, in charge of the execution of the conciliar decrees concerning the liturgy. It regularly publishes *notitiae,* referred to by the author in this article.

evitable difficulties and questions—but also to prepare the people for them, to introduce and to explain them. The resulting reflection has had an influence in depth which the Constitution by itself could not have brought about, but which the Instruction, as the first step in the direction of application, was bound to achieve. From all kinds of practical situations there arose questions about the basis, the purpose and the perspectives of this liturgical renewal. The answers to these questions could not be lifted, ready-made, from the text of the Constitution, and we are far from having finished with them.

In the many periodicals that deal with liturgy from the pastoral point of view, we see that these questions, directly inspired by practical needs, become more and more relevant. It is indeed not enough to explain the contents and background of the new regulations and directives, to discuss the problems involved (such as the matter of translations), and to suggest the best ways and means of implementing them. All this is necessary, but it is not all that is necessary. We have to realize that the first rather drastic innovations in the liturgy, which were announced as the heralds of a series of further innovations, have created a new situation, of which we can hardly grasp the full extent and depth.

Practically everywhere people use the loose expression, "the new liturgy". Now it is obvious that one can object to this phrase because it implies, ultimately, a certain confusion between liturgy and liturgical forms, between liturgy and rubrics. Whatever the variety or changes affecting the celebration of the liturgy, as long as it is the act of worship of the Mystical Body of Christ, Head and members,[3] it is and remains the same. And yet one may well ask whether the expression objected to does not show a profound sense of realism. For many people, the "image" of the liturgy is destroyed, insofar as this "image" is very different from a theological definition or an abstract idea, in that it refers to the practical expression of an idea that we incorporate into our concrete existence. And this applies even more to those for

[3] Cf. *The Constitution on the Sacred Liturgy* (Glen Rock, N.J.: Paulist Press, 1965), Art. 7.

whom the changes introduced by the Instruction mean something more than a change in the rubrics—a change which may go a little farther than on previous occasions; they regard it as a first attempt at driving home the fact that the liturgy is concerned not with things, but with people,[4] that the liturgy does not consist in norms, rules and regulations, however necessary, or in impressive and venerable ceremonies, but rather in the celebrating community of the faithful.

However familiar we may already have become with this idea through theological reflection and reading what for so many years has already been written and said about it, the real impact of this idea has only come about through the practical application of the innovations. And this is why the old "image" which still prevailed in spite of everything, though perhaps no longer so completely, has now been destroyed in actual fact. We shall all experience this sooner or later when the liturgical renewal is put into practice in the right spirit. What is disturbing is not the fact itself, the inevitable, not yet fully grasped, consequence of the renewal; it is rather that the new "image", for which we are all searching, may drive out important or even essential elements, or at least push them into the background. In order to meet this danger, it is not enough to refer to the Constitution. However admirable this document may be and however indispensable its directives, it is not meant and not suited to convey this new and concrete "image" by its very nature and origin.

It has become somewhat fashionable to describe the Constitution on the Sacred Liturgy like its predecessor *Mediator Dei,* as the *Magna Carta* of the liturgical movement and of the liturgical renewal of the Church. Perhaps we would be more discreet in the use of this term if we realized that the *Magna Carta* of 1215 was a "bulwark of freedom" forced by the nobility and the people upon a king who drifted to absolutism. Since then the expression has no doubt lost some of its revolutionary color, and

---

[4] F. Morlot, "Une condition prealable à toute formation liturgique: un changement de mentalité," in *Maison-Dieu* 78 (1964²), p. 7: "La liturgie, ce ne sont pas des choses, ce sont des personnes."

it is taken in our context as an indication of the fact that the Constitution—even more than the encyclical—is a document that
inaugurates a new ecclesial polity. It is a declaration of principle,
illustrated with a number of practical norms,[5] written in a style
of its own.[6] One cannot use and interpret it in the usual juridical
manner. If we want to emphasize and assess its juridical character, we shall have to look for it rather in the direction of constitutional law which has its own peculiar background and rules
for interpretation[7] determined by its purpose and its origin.

Insofar as this last point is concerned, we must remember that
the Constitution is not the work of one man, or even of a homogeneous group. As Vagaggini rightly points out: "The fact that
the texts of Vatican Council II are the fruit of very extensive,
truly worldwide collaboration, is an enormous advantage. But it
also has occasional disadvantages: the texts have often passed
through too many hands; sometimes they lack in unity where the
editing is concerned, and they are often the result of a large
amount of compromise." [8] Even in the Constitution one notices
here and there certain tensions deriving from opposing views
or the nature of the liturgy itself, which, like the Church, contains a paradox.[9]

Without in any way belittling the value of this conciliar document or showing any lack of respect for it, we may hope neverthe-

[5] Cf. Art. 3.

[6] Cf. P.-M. Gy in *Maison-Dieu* 76 (1962[4]), pp. 12-3; see also the
remarks of A. M. Roguet in the commentary in *Maison-Dieu* 77 (1964[1]),
pp. 10-1.

[7] J. Bigordá Montmany, "Estilo jurídico de la Constitución," in *Phase*
4 (1964), p. 150: "The Constitution on the Sacred Liturgy must be
understood in terms of constitutional law, and should be interpreted in
accordance with the criteria governing this field of law. This is the implicit
and explicit intention that can be seen in its whole structure. This conviction arises spontaneously from a reflective reading and lengthy study
of this magnificent document."

[8] C. Vagaggini, "Lo spirito della Costituzione sulla Liturgia," in *Riv.
Lit.* 51 (1964), p. 47.

[9] F. Morlot, *loc. cit.*, n. 3, p. 20: "The Church is a living paradox, and
the liturgy shares that aspect." The author then proceeds to develop this
paradox under the following headings: community and institution; body
and spirit; initiative and obedience; and, lastly, unity and diversity.

less that the Constitution will not be taken and handled as the last word on what the liturgy is and must become, and that it will not suffer the fate of the decrees of the Council of Trent which the theologians considered for several centuries to be the complete epitome of the whole tradition of the Church.[10] We particularly hope this is true in regard to the very important section on "The Nature of the Sacred Liturgy and Its Importance in the Church's Life" (Arts. 5-13) which has rightly been praised in all the commentaries and yet which is not wholly satisfactory when one takes a closer look at it. Fr. Morlot has aptly described the proper character of the liturgy: "As the action of men at prayer, the liturgy presupposes a definite anthropology; as a religious service directed toward God, it expresses a theology; as a Christian service, it depends on christology and ecclesiology." [11] There is no doubt that the Constitution does justice to the last three elements (theology, christology and ecclesiology), particularly when we remember that the Constitution on the Sacred Liturgy preceded the dogmatic Constitution on the Church, but one cannot escape the impression that too little attention has been paid to anthropology; this could lead to misunderstanding or to a one-sided elucidation of the liturgy.

When, for example, M. Garrido declares that the primary and principal law of the liturgy is the law of objectivity, and that the liturgy is the way toward salvation determined by God and not by man,[12] his statements can, of course, be understood and explained correctly, but one wonders whether this view leaves enough room for the human contribution to the liturgy. This

[10] Cf. G. Alberigo, "The Council of Trent: New Views on the Occasion of Its Fourth Centenary," in *Concilium* 7: *Historical Problems of Church Renewal* (1965), pp. 69-87.

[11] F. Morlot, *loc. cit.*, p. 19.

[12] M. Garrido, "Naturaleza de la liturgia en la constitución litúrgica del Concilio Vaticano Segundo," in *Liturgia* (Burgos) 19 (1964), p. 164. "But the first law, which dominates the whole concept of liturgy, is the law of objectivity; the road by which we can and must go to God has not been left to man's free choice, still less his whim; God himself has worked it out for us. Our salvation can only be accomplished if we follow that road, if we accept it and adapt ourselves to God."

last point gives rise to many demands in the concrete shaping of the liturgy, demands of which we become more and more conscious as we try to put this liturgical renewal into practice.

Therefore, it is vital that we continue to reconsider the matter, particularly at present. These questions today preoccupy many priests engaged in pastoral work, and they can perhaps be reduced to one basic question: "What kind of liturgy are we aiming at?" One can, of course, brush this question aside as a futile or even presumptuous attempt to foresee the future and simply say that we can leave this with all confidence to the guidance of the Church. However, such an answer will probably satisfy no one, and rightly so, because the pattern of what we expect in the future is bound to determine the spirit in which the present innovations are conducted and in which the faithful are being educated.

The terms of reference given by the Council to the Commission for the Implementation of the Constitution on the Sacred Liturgy can obviously be interpreted in various ways. For the future it is possible that a liturgy is envisaged which will be brought up-to-date, renewed, decentralized and thus more pluriform, but which will basically remain as tightly regulated as in the past. It even seems probable that many fathers who voted in favor of the Constitution actually held this view. But such a liturgy would not correspond to the purposes laid down by the Constitution itself for this liturgical renewal. Such a tight regulation cannot possibly be deduced from the theology of the liturgy. It conflicts with the demands of a liturgy as the vital expression of the contribution of the faithful (which also belongs to the essence of the liturgy), and it is highly questionable from the point of view of tradition.[13] P.-M. Gy's interpretation of these terms of reference is therefore much more acceptable. The way in which these terms of reference are formulated, he says,

---

[13] Cf. P.-M. Gy, "Entre hier et demain; tradition et progrès, initiative et fidélité," in *Maison-Dieu* 80 (1964⁴), pp. 217-26; G. Pinckers, "Pourquoi le Moyen-Age a-t-il uniformisé les rites liturgiques?" in *Paroisse et Liturgie* 47 (1965), pp. 25-35; M. C. Vanhengel, "De celebrerende priester en de heiligende symboliek der sacramenten," in *Tijdschrift voor Theologie* 3 (1963), pp. 111-38, esp. pp. 123-6.

"expresses the desire for greater elasticity and a certain variety, together with the determination that unity will not suffer. The Commission must try, in a gradual, practical and therefore pastoral manner, to bring about a progressive relaxation of uniformity while seeing to it that unity is not harmed thereby".[14] Here he thinks particularly of two lines along which this can be achieved: by leaving freedom of choice in a fair number of cases in the matter of choosing texts, formulas or pericopes, and by indicating various possibilities in the rubrics themselves, as has in fact been done already in the Instruction and in the rite for concelebration.[15] In this connection it is both significant and promising that the Consilium, in one of its many unofficial replies, defends this freedom on exactly the grounds that the liturgical celebration must be something live for living human beings.[16]

This is obviously not the last word in this matter. The interpretation of liturgical law and the practice of obedience connected with it have been the subject of a frank discussion in a special number of the periodical *Paroisse et Liturgie*[17] which provoked a rather sharp reply from the Belgian bishops.[18] Indeed, a number of statements made by some authors are debatable and might lead to premature conclusions at cross-purposes with the legitimate guidance of the ecclesiastical authorities. Nevertheless, the questions put here are real questions; they should not be stifled in silence and they must be given a satisfactory answer

[14] P.-M. Gy, *ibid.*, p. 222.

[15] *Ibid.*, pp. 222-3.

[16] *Notitiae* 1 (1965), p. 254: "Can the competent territorial authority for a whole region, or the bishop for his diocese, lay down one single practice to be followed by all, in order to achieve uniformity? REPLY: Taken in itself, yes. Nevertheless, he should beware of not destroying that freedom, foreseen by the new rubrics, of adapting the rite *in an intelligent way* to the Church or the congregation so that the sacred rite as a whole be something alive for living human beings."

[17] *Paroisse et Liturgie* 47 (1965), n. 1: "De l'obéissance en matière liturgique."

[18] The letter of the Belgian bishops to the editors of *Paroisse et Liturgie* has been published in that periodical, together with the editors' reply (*ibid.*, n. 3, before p. 241).

someday if the renewal of the liturgy is not to remain suspended in mid-air.

Lastly, I want to mention an article by G. Hasenhüttel where the general problem of the future of the liturgy is treated differently.[19] This article deserves a more detailed analysis, but I have to limit myself to a few remarks. There are very many of the faithful (whom we must indeed describe as "faithful" but who are not "religious"), to whom a religious service and a liturgy that are not contemporary and outside the experience of life do not appeal. "The Council fathers had no wish to condemn such people but would rather tell them that the liturgy will be renewed, will no longer be a closed territory, but will rather lead to the sanctification of every event of daily life."[20] On the basis of article 61 of the Constitution, he pleads for a liturgy really close to life and not alien to it. The problem raised by the author which lies behind his argument leads to many more questions, and it is perhaps difficult to agree wholly with what the author says. But there is no doubt that the author tackles a live contemporary issue and what he says deserves to be studied more closely.

I intended this article as a report on the literature which has appeared in connection with the Constitution and the corresponding Instruction. In actuality, it has turned out to be a number of personal remarks and observations prompted by a few—too few —articles, and it does not in any way pretend to be complete. Even as such, I hope it may still serve a useful purpose.

[19] G. Hasenhüttel, "Die Konstitution über die heilige Liturgie; eine theologische Besinnung," in *Bibel u. Liturgie* 38 (1964/5), pp. 187-92.
[20] *Ibid.*, p. 189.

Helmut Hucke/*Neu-Isenburg, W. Germany*

Introduction:
New Church Music
in the Vernacular

In the practical implementation of the liturgical reform, the problem of church music will play a large part, and perhaps the largest part. For singing is—after communion—the most interior of the ways and means for the community to participate in the liturgy. Nearly all the rites by which the people become active in the liturgical solemnities, and the greater part of the rites in which the liturgy addresses the people, pose the problem of whether and in what way they will be sung. With regard to singing, in hardly any other respect is the liturgical reform faced with such a large practical task. In many places there has been, up to now, very little singing, or even none at all. And where people have been singing during the liturgical celebrations, it is perhaps still somewhat difficult to admit that this singing is liturgical. The reform of church music in the liturgy cannot be the work of the clergy and the specialists alone; it must spring from the labor of the whole community and from each member.

The church music of the liturgical reform will continue to be of international importance; the problems that will crop up from one country to another, from one language to another, will in general be the same. What has been hitherto sung in Latin will not constitute a fixed blueprint for what may be sung in the vernacular. These premises will illuminate our understanding of

the nature and foundation of sacred music, and lead to the creation of new forms of this music. Moreover, international communication will be used as never before in the history of sacred
music. The implementation of the renewal in church music in
particular instances will here and there stem from different premises and demand different solutions, but the overall principles will
be the same. Even the recent past shows how much the initiatives
which have been set on foot, the new forms of liturgical chant
in the mother tongue, can bring about: they will have a revolutionary effect and will bring about the removal of differences
of speech and nationality. An example is the case of the French
psalms of J. Gelineau! Perhaps we may dare to hope that our
church music will also be enriched from lands where the Church
is still in her youth, as the sacred music of the 4th century and
of medieval Europe was enriched by the hymnody of the East
and of the Germanic peoples, respectively.

The following bibliographical survey of books and articles cannot give a complete picture; it must remain in essence a sum-
mary. The real state of affairs is to be seen in the works of church
music rather than in things written about them. Therefore, it is
necessary to include works of church music in this bibliographical
survey. Hence, we have here an initial installment which will be
continued in the future.

In the following account will be found a survey of the requirements underlying church music and the new vernacular publications in the field according to category. In the next volume of
Concilium (Vol. 22, 1967) devoted to the liturgy, the account
will be extended over a wider area.

Réné Reboud/*Amiens, France*

Sacred Music
for the People:
France since World War II

At the close of the war, the situation of popular sacred music in France was as follows: the parishes had at their disposal two kinds of hymns:

1. The traditional repertoire which included (a) some French choral pieces, both old and new, in the manner of Goudimel and, to some extent, his contemporaries; (b) some old missionary hymns, from Maunoir, Surin, de Montfort, etc. Their theology was solid, although their music and text were perhaps a bit elementary. De Montfort once wrote:

> *Voici mes vers et mes chansons*
> *S'ils ne sont pas beaux, ils sont bons*
> *S'ils ne flattent pas les oreilles*
> *Ils riment de grandes merveilles*[1]

(c) the many works of the Jesuit Lambillotte, and of his followers, who built upon 19th-century operatic forms; (d) romantic inspirational hymns, such as Lamartine's:

> *Ah! qui me donnera des paroles ardentes*
> *Des paroles du ciel, une langue de feu*

---

[1] Here are my songs and simple words,
Their beauty scant, their value sure;
If they seem harsh, keep in mind
Their rimes recount great wonders.

95

> *Une angélique voix et des levres brûlantes*
> *Pour te bénir, mon Dieu*[2]

or Gounod's:

> *Le Ciel a visité la terre*
> *Mon Bien-aimé repose en moi*[3]

2. Hymns "in keeping with the *motu proprio*" (*ad mentem motu proprio*). Many composers responded to the appeal of St. Pius X and produced hymns in the musical and literary style of the *Belle Epoque*. Many fine turns of phrase, pleasant nuances and refined emotions were to be found in these works so characteristic of their age. One no longer heard the Blessed Virgin being addressed in Lhande's words:

> *Ton nom si doux, ton sourire ingénu*[4]

and the music of La Tombelle no longer suited the words of Jesus:

> *Laissez venir à moi les tout-petits enfants*[5]

and one despaired, with Canon Besse, of ever detecting the theological train of thought in this hymn to the Sacred Heart:

> *O Gloire de la Trinité*
> *A qui le Fils doit son essence*
> *Le Saint-Esprit sa pureté*
> *Et le Père sa complaisance*[6]

[2] Ah! who shall give me fiery words,
Heavenly words and tongue of flame,
Angelic voice and burning lips
To bless you, my God.
[3] Heaven came to call upon the earth
My well-beloved now rests within me.
[4] The sweetness of your name, your open smile.
[5] Let the little children be, and do not hinder them
from coming to me.
[6] O Glory of the Trinity,
To whom the Son owes his essence,
The Holy Spirit his purity,
The Father his good pleasure.
(Cf. C. Besse, *Vieux cantiques, Nouvelles romances.*)

One delightful and successful work was the litany "O Vierge Marie" in a setting by the Abbé Brun. Much more was needed.

From the years 1935-1936 French Christians have needed something new in sacred music. Some collections of hymns had already attempted a better selection of titles and the composition of new hymns, but there was not much stylistic change, as can be seen in the collections of Pirio (Vannes), Delporte (Lille) and Besnier (Nantes). They performed a great service and continue to do so, but the true origin of the new hymns is to be found in the youth movements. Joseph Folliet made the songs of young German Catholics widely known; Doncoeur and his movement provided a reeducation in song for young Frenchmen; the Abbé Reboud, inspired by Fillère, wrote the first works for the liturgy of the people in the youthful city of Jouy sur Morin. The Abbé David Julien will soon rejoin this group.

Most of these works were not hymns, strictly speaking, but idealistic songs inspired by the songs of political movements where French youths were given the opportunity to sing of their faith. But there rapidly developed an urgent need for songs to be incorporated into a vital liturgy; this moved in the direction of what may be called the "new hymn".

Shortly after the war, a religious revival, the Great Conversion (*le Grand Retour*), raced through the French provinces. It remained faithful to the traditional repertoire in an imperfect manner, but it was known to one and all. Their songs came out of the 19th century: I am a Christian, Queen of France, speak, command and govern. The result was good, but it was clear that the *Grand Retour* would witness the last great period of the traditional hymn. The first National Congress of CPL (held at Saint-Flour in 1945) and the second (held at Lyons in 1947) brought out the general wish for a more scriptural, more liturgical music that would invite the participation of all those assisting at the service.

After the Congress in Lyons an inquiry was launched that resulted in the publication of a special issue of the journal

Musique et Liturgie (4-5, 1948). It was made up of a remarkable study by Gelineau on the problem of popular sacred music. It is interesting to reread this article today. From the outset, Gelineau set himself upon a pastoral terrain and endeavored to organize the hymns then in use. He first categorized the melodies and then the texts, according to criteria that he would perhaps be reluctant to employ now, as we shall see later. He further distinguished (1) Gregorian melodies, (2) metrical melodies, (3) choral pieces, (4) folksongs, (5) classical melodies, (6) the traditional hymn, and (7) modern compositions. The texts were also broken down as follows: (1) ancient, (2) traditional, (3) hymns of the 20th century.

For the future, Gelineau, after paying his respects to these first efforts, brought out some new texts that would, in the spirit of the liturgy, lead to new missionary hymns, new hymns for the Mass, hymns for the liturgical seasons, hymns for the promotion of sacramental and community life, and psalms within reach of the people's ability. On the subject of the psalms, two supports were sketched out that would later give us "the Gelineau psalms" which, in 1948, were still only in embryo. He insisted then on the need for style, on the genres that one could make use of (he employed terms that have today become commonplace, such as the *genre responsorial*), and he insisted too on the importance of a fixed metrical pattern (*isorythmie*). His conclusions were forthright: (1) "Nearly all the desirable texts for French religious music are still to be created"; (2) "Many of the best known melodies, and many others not so widely known, should be kept and published without doing harm to the endeavors of new works." Gelineau concludes with an appeal for a popular repertoire and an edition for the people.

Seventeen Years Later

Seventeen years after this article, we can reflect upon the direction taken. It was effected in several stages. One of the most important was the introduction of the psalms sung in French, which followed closely the publication of the Jerusalem Bible.

The translators of the psalter (Gelineau among them) had taken great pains to retain in the translated text the same strophic and rhythmic structure that they found in the original Hebrew. This was a wonderful discovery—the recognition that, without great difficulty, the psalter could be sung in French without chopping up the sacred text into small verses and without losing the unity of the strophe. The method used was based upon the recurrence of rhythmical stresses that one may find listening to children sing "Frère Jacques": whatever the number of syllables in a verse, there are never more than two rhythmical stresses; if there are a great number of syllables, they simply pass over them very quickly—a technique that Gerard Manley Hopkins called "sprung rhythm".

This sung translation of the psalms has been an enormous success. It has opened up the psalter to the Christian people and has excited the interest of musicians in the psalter—and not just "to improve upon Gelineau". There have also been some psalms in French composed by Geoffray, Sanson (exalted music!), Julien (more popular), Jacques Berthier (author of many of the compositions sung at Taizé), and even, based on another translation, Ireneu Segarra (Montserrat).

Some Composers

Lucien Deiss deserves special mention for the scope and warmth of his work. Hymns, psalms, recitatives, responsories—Deiss has a personal, deeply apostolic style; the scriptural passages are chosen with great care. Harmonics are very important in his naturally polyphonic compositions. Deiss, like Gelineau, has many imitators.

The Abbé David Julien writes in a style that has gained wide popular acceptance; his music is best heard when performed before large audiences. His language is simple and forthright. Like the Abbé Reboud, he has taken young people's songs and adapted them for the liturgy.

A fine group has been organized in Lyons around the Editions du Chalet; in it are Servel and the Abbé Robert Marthouret.

They have compiled many hymns in a style at once youthful and traditional, displaying a joyous and lively religious conviction. Also working in Lyons is Claude Rozier, one of the better composers in this school.

Certain famous musicians have been working hand in hand with Church musicians, among them Gaston Litaize, Jean Bonfils, César Geoffray, and Jean Langlais (whose work is most significant). Stylists such as Barjon, Daniel Hameline and the poet Jean-Claude Renard, have worked together on the texts.

Everyone I have named, and others I have neglected to mention (to avoid turning this article into a bland directory), have composed thousands of works whose overall value is admittedly uneven. But the method of publishing sheet music and allowing their compositions to be purchased, at minimum expense, one by one, has given everyone the opportunity to assemble a collection of the most suitable pieces. Works of lesser value will disappear entirely, while the good ones will rise to the top; little by little a national repertoire will be established. This method of publication and distribution could only be realized through the goodwill of interested publishers.

Another important stage in the production, inspiration and control of new sacred music for the people has been the establishment of the journal *Eglise qui Chante*. Most of the names mentioned above can be found among its contributors. It is the organ of the *Association Saint Ambroise,* dedicated to sacred music for the people, and of its affiliated branches in Belgium (ABSA) and in Canada (ACSA). These are places where those who work in the musical realm may meet, study, converse and establish rapport for their cooperative ventures.

Another influential development has been the cooperative edition of a collection called *Cantiques et Psaumes* containing the best new music and some of the best old works. It is sold inexpensively without music, and a printing of more than two million copies has made for widespread distribution. This has been a strong contribution toward the creation of a national repertoire mentioned above.

The Present

The light illuminating all this work has continually changed color since the appearance of the Constitution on the Sacred Liturgy. There is no longer any question simply of "composing hymns", but rather of creating music for the renewed liturgy. In the meantime, there is a need for reflection upon the function of music in Christian worship and, further, upon the repercussions of this function on musical structure (*Sanctus, Gradual,* etc.). Gelineau would no doubt no longer classify musical pieces according to their melody and the origin of their melody, but rather according to their use in worship: processionals, litanies, recitatives, psalms, hymns, acclamations. What was once called the Ordinary of the Mass tends to come apart, with each musical piece making a unit of the part of the Mass to which it belongs: *Kyrie*/Litany, *Gloria*/Hymn, *Credo*/Recitative, *Sanctus*/Acclamation, *Agnus Dei*/Litany.

Now that the Constitution on the Sacred Liturgy has bestowed a new dignity upon French music, making it enter into the fullness of the liturgy, French musicians have no intention of falling short of their obligations. Far from underestimating the work of those who preceded them, they shall endeavor, humbly yet boldly, to stand upon their shoulders in order to see farther than their predecessors. Faithful to the instructions of the Church, they wish to remain "filled with the Christian spirit", and to fully understand "that they have been called to cultivate sacred music and increase its store of treasures" (Constitution on the Sacred Liturgy, Art. 121).

Erhard Quack/*Speyer, W. Germany*

Music for Divine Worship in the German Language

Church music in the vernacular has played a significant role in Germany for many hundreds of years. For the most part, divine worship has been carried out with hymns in the German language. In many communities this was the only form in which the people joined in the singing of church music, but this participation took place alongside rather than inside the liturgy. Hence, the liturgical movement has endeavored to exert a wide influence on church music during the last decade.

The liturgical reform initiated by the Council has been the means by which church music has been given full liberty, in view of its great and long-standing influence. But the reform also calls for a plan that will put an end to an exclusively Latin tradition. Therefore it is not surprising that many new phenomena have appeared.

One problem at the heart of the new liturgical chant centers around liturgical *recitative* in the German language. It also poses the question of a German psalmody which, in the case of new compositions, is a central one. Around it are grouped the chants for the *Proper of the Mass* and for the canonical hours. A further problem is the congregational singing of the prose texts of the *Ordinary of the Mass*. Finally, we must also keep in mind the question of preserving the rich treasury of German hymns

103

for the liturgical feasts. Therefore, for the purposes of our survey, we have the following groups: (1) orations, epistles, and acclamations, (2) psalmody, (3) chants for the *Proper,* (4) the canonical hours, (5) the *Common of the Mass,* and (6) hymns.

1. The question of *liturgical recitative* could be given a preliminary solution. On the basis of a proclamation of the Bishop of Limburg, instructions were given to the Liturgical Institute of Trier to select and to rework old and new formulas for *recitative.* These were approved by the Bishops' conference at Fulda. We now have two melodies for the orations and five for the epistle and Gospel, of which about half are derived from the old Roman melodies; the others are the work of contemporary composers. They are being published anonymously in an uninterrupted series for the entire liturgical year.[1] A clear synopsis of the melodies with examples, rules for applying them, and the theory behind them is soon to appear in book form.[2] With these melodies there will appear at the same time for the lector, in German, the *Pater Noster* and the approved melody for the *Libera nos.*[3]

2. The effort to draw up a *German psalmody* proceeds, in the main, in two directions: (a) psalm-tunes according to the Gregorian method, or Gregorian models changed to match speech rhythm, and (b) the creation of a new psalmody with its own modes and a rhythmically shaped *recitative.*

(a) German Gregorian psalmody long ago deviated from being a literal transference of the Roman melodies. It avoids monotony and selects those forms that can be accommodated to the word accent without too much difficulty. An extensive systematic edition and a complete German Gregorian Psalter are still awaited. Publication is taking place for the most part in

[1] *Orationen und Lesungen zur Feier der hl. Eucharistie,* four numbers now out (Freiburg: Christophorus).

[2] *Kommentar zu den approbierten Orations—und Lesetönen,* edited by the Liturgical Institute, Trier (Mainz: Grunewald; Freiburg: Christophorus).

[3] *Priestergesänge zur Feier der hl. Eucharistie; Vaterunserblatt für die Gemeinde* (Freiburg: Christophorus).

connection with the *Proper of the Mass* or the canonical hours and will be mentioned in the proper place.

(b) The comprehensive attempt at a new psalmody is presented in *Neues Psalmenbuch*.[4] It consists of seventy-two psalms and canticles presented as responsories to be sung. The strophic arrangement of the psalms has been carried out according to the new modes for *recitative* with cantor and choir leading, and after each strophe with a pause at the end of the refrain, the congregation answers. By the addition of more refrains, it is possible to change each psalm to suit the different liturgical situations (*Mass, Matins, Vigil*). Where there is the possibility of singing either in unison or in polyphony, adaptation can be made to situations as the need arises. Other editions such as the *Deutscher Singpsalter*[5] and *Gesänge zur Eucharistiefeier*[6] arrange the psalmody on the model of J. Gelineau's work. The step-wise *recitative* cannot, however, do justice to the differing speech-rhythms unless the accentuation can be handled in a uniform fashion.

3. The psalmody is part and parcel of the *Proper of the Mass*. Among German editions must be named first those that include the whole ecclesiastical cycle. Of these the greater part are collections of the Sundays in their seasonal groupings. H. Kahlefeld's *Gesänge für den Gottesdienst*[7] are written in German Gregorian style; structurally, it is an exemplary work, but musically it is little more than an imitation. *Singende Gemeinde*[8] give the antiphons of the Gregorian psalmody in song-like para-

---

[4] *Neues Psalmenbuch*, edited by H. Hucke, E. Quack, and K. Schmidthüs; editions for cantor, choir, and organ (separately); text for congregation (text and refrains); collaborators: F. Doppelbauer, B. Hummel, K. Marx, E. Pfiffner, F. Schieri, et al. (Freiburg: Christophorus). Records also available.

[5] *Deutscher Singpsalter*, ed. L. Drees (Munich: J. Pfeiffer).

[6] *Gesänge zur Eucharistiefeier* (33 numbers), ed. B. Senger (Dülmen: Laumann).

[7] *Gesänge für den Gottesdienst* (2 volumes), ed. H. Kahlefeld (Munich: Kösel).

[8] *Singende Gemeinde* (10 numbers), ed. H. Klein, with M. Thurmair and H. Rohr (Freiburg: Christophorus).

phrase. In *Singendes Gottesvolk,*[9] parts of songs are often used as main themes. A certain "folksiness" is here attained by means that, musically speaking, are questionable. The collection *Gesänge zur Eucharistiefeier*[10] seeks to speak to the community through a primitiveness bordering on simplicity in rhythm and melody.

In individual editions there are orchestrated compositions for the *Common* as well as for the *Proper of the Season:* in modern homophone settings there is a *Messe für das Jahr* by R. Thomas,[11] a German *Proper* by G. Ratzinger,[12] German *Psalm-Masses* by G. Fässler and Gr. Müller,[13] and the distinguished *Propers for Corpus Christi, the Feast of the Most Holy Trinity,* and for *Good Friday* of F. Schieri;[14] in more conventional style H. Lemachers has a *Proper for the Epiphany*[15] and W. Waldbroel a *Midnight* (first) *Mass for Christmas.*[16] The German Masses for *Corpus Christi,* for the *Feast of the Sacred Heart,* and for the *Feasts of the Blessed Virgin Mary* give the *Propers* in simple melody for singing in unison; they are by F. Fleckenstein (cf. note 12).

Here should be mentioned scattered examples of liturgical music which have found their way into use in the course of the liturgical year. H. Schroeder has written new melodies for the *Passion* according to Matthew and according to John.[17] Here, too, is the *Passion* according to Matthew of Suriano for voice and choral responses.[18] F. Schieri has the hymns for the *Mandatum* and for the *Easter Vigil,* for choir and congregation with modern organ accompaniment (cf. note 14). J. Ahrens has the

[9] *Singendes Gottesvolk,* edited by N. Föhr and H. Sabel (Trier: Paulinus).

[10] *Gebetsrufe und Psalmen* (Rottenburg: diocesan publication).

[11] Munich: Church of St. Ludwig, pastoral publication. Records available.

[12] Altötting: Coppenrath.

[13] Lucerne: Cron.

[14] Munich: Uni-Druck. Records available.

[15] Augsburg: Böhm & Son.

[16] Heidelberg: Süddeutscher Musikverlag W. Müller.

[17] Düsseldorf: Schwann.

[18] Freiburg: Christophorus.

music for the *Easter Vigil* in a sophisticated choral style (cf. note 16). K. Seckinger has four-part interludes for the ecclesiastical year (cf. note 12).

4. *German psalmody* is to be found primarily in the editions of the canonical hours. Many of the new diocesan hymnbooks have the *Vespers* in German for the principal feasts and the various seasons of the ecclesiastical year. The selection of the psalms does not keep strictly to the rubrics of the liturgy and for the most part is content with inferior numbers. The antiphons are often dispensed with. Gregorian models are more or less well adapted. The *Compline* and *Vespers for Sunday* of the Liturgical Institute of Trier have been issued independently (cf. note 18). H. Kahlefeld has—apart from the *Vespers* and *Compline*—also arranged *Matins* for Christmas and for Good Friday.[19] The aforementioned complete edition of the psalms (cf. note 4) makes it possible to have in place the *Vespers, Matins,* etc., and to make use of the book for the new choral needs.

5. *The Ordinary of the Mass* is also given new and wide scope in the new liturgical music. With regard to text editions we may distinguish three different groups: (a) the *Ordinary of the Mass* with complete wording; (b) the *Ordinary* with some small variations in the text; (c) the *Ordinary of the Mass* in song-like paraphrase.

Because a new translation of the text of the *Ordinary* into German is still awaited, many composers are holding off. For the old uniform text there are available the following compositions: *Gemeindegesänge der heiligen Messe,* five *Ordinaries* by H. Rohr (cf. note 18), which in its structure is still very much influenced by the Gregorian melody, with text shared by the schola and the congregation. A new series, *Fünf deutsche Ordinarien,*[20] is rhythmically and melodically song-like in structure; the same is true, too, of the compositions for the Cathedral of

---

[19] Munich: Kösel.
[20] *Fünf deutsche Ordinarien* by H. Schubert, E. Sorge, G. Trexler, H. Schroeder, R. Bisegger; R. Ewerhart, ed. (Münster: Orbis).

Augsburg written by K. Kraft (cf. note 15). Side by side with these compositions for voices in unison are the polyphonic *Masses* of W. Hierdeis and J. Monter (cf. note 15) which deserve attention as examples of contemporary compositions, but which are not in line with the intention of the liturgical reform since they exclude the congregation from the singing.

In Group B are included, by reason of their pronounced rhythmic and melodic character and modern tonality, the *Deutsche Ordinariumsmesse* of F. Schieri (cf. note 18) and the simple choral arrangement of the compositions written for the Cathedral of Mainz by H. Rohr (cf. note 18). In the *Mass* with congregational acclamations by E. Quack (cf. note 18), the people's part is limited to short responses so as to enable them to participate in songs of greater scope. In the three last-named *Ordinaries* the choir's part may be sung either in unison or in several voices.

In Group C the last decade has seen the production of a large number of musical texts for the *Ordinary* that probably will not survive the liturgical reform because of their unsatisfactory texts. A sound direction for the musical settings for the *Ordinary* has been begun in the brief *E-Mass* and followed in the series of *Ordinaries* to be found in *Singenden Gemeinde* (cf. note 18). However, here too the critic must continue to discriminate until worthwhile results are forthcoming.

6. *Preserving and increasing the treasury of good sacred music in the German language* for use in divine worship is one of the most urgent needs of church musicians in Germany. Besides the music necessary at Mass, there are the psalm tones and the music for the festal seasons. In *33 Psalmlieder* (cf. note 18) there are original treatments in good new translations by Kaspar Ulenberg; these are now more widely accessible. With the limitation to a small number of melodies, the *Liedpsalter* (cf. note 17) seeks to attain the same end. As books to be used for singing the *Proper,* these editions are especially worthwhile. To them should be added the polyphonic settings of Lasso, Hagius, et al., which are particularly noteworthy. Polyphonic

collections of our church music, from simple voice-settings to lied-motets, are an essential part of the choral repertoire and are used for all antiphonal singing with the congregation. All publishers are taking pains to issue them.

The kinds of singing for the choir and the hymns for the people, as well as music for the organ and other instruments, deserve special consideration because in them, through varied arrangements and different distributions of voices in the stanzas, original and yet "folksy" forms of musicianship for use in the church have been created. We can name only some representatives from the multitude that have recently appeared on the market: *Giestliche Liedkantaten* (nine numbers) by E. Bonitz, H. Schubert, E. Pfiffner, E. Woll, et al.;[21] *Kleine Liedkantaten* by Doppelbauer, Tittel, et al. (cf. note 12); *Liedkantaten* by H. Lemacher and H. Schroeder (cf. note 17). The worth of these compositions is uneven and ranges from unpretentious mediocrity to high art. Worth mentioning also are the hymns assembled and arranged by J. Dahmen after the settings of the old masters (cf. note 18).

Large compositions of sacred music cannot be mentioned in this survey which has been limited to music for divine worship. The center of gravity of the new work is, for the time being, the immediate need for liturgical music. But it is to be hoped that from wholesome congregational singing, in unison and in simple polyphonic compositions, our age will provide a means for the highest forms of sacred music which, even if not an integral part of the liturgy, will find a place in the churches.

[21] Regensburg: Pustet.

Stephen Mbunga/*Peramiho, Tanzania*

Church Music in Tanzania

In spite of all upheavals and storms of the wind of change, Tanzanian culture—including music—is still predominantly African. While it may be remarkable how rapidly the human type is modified or transformed by a new way of life or a new environment, it is nevertheless true that, even in the midst of these changes, the cultural tradition of a people remains predominant. Even if this tradition were distorted, a nation will have the pride to reconstruct itself and to return to the integrity of indigenous capabilities, thereby doing justice to its distinctive national attributes.

Hence, African music is the indispensable basis for the development of Tanzanian church music, although it may seem unlikely, in view of the influences from abroad, that *a pure African* church music will evolve in Tanzania.

Nor should it be overlooked that Tanzanian culture is intimately related to religion. This culture manifests a uniformity in its common conception of life, standards of behavior and values. Tanzanians have always regarded *their individual life and the life of society as intimately dependent on forces* that lie outside their own control—*on superhuman powers* that rule both the world and the life of man.

Here we can find the right link between Tanzanian church music and Tanzanian culture. Analysis of the majority of the songs connected with these ceremonies and rituals shows that they are textually impregnated with striking religious sentiments and philosophy, even if the songs were not meant specifically for divine cult in the Western sense.

Thus, the Church will show wisdom in helping Tanzania to *keep her old musical inheritance,* her birthright, as well as contributing, by the *establishment of good new traditions,* to the organic growth and welfare of the nation. Only then shall Tanzanians "know of a verity that it is idle mendicancy to discard one's own and beg for the foreign, and at the same time they shall feel that it is the extreme abjectness of poverty to dwarf oneself by rejecting the foreign".[1]

In the effort, which must follow Vatican Council II, to reconstitute the liturgy as the "font" and "summit" of Christian life, the Constitution on the Sacred Liturgy stresses that the popular religious music and "singing by the people is to be skillfully fostered, so that in devotions and sacred exercises, as also during liturgical services, the voices of the faithful may ring out according to the norms and requirements of the rubrics".[2] *Worship and pastoral work must regulate Church music.* In other words, "One should not begin from a repertoire or from established musical works but with the liturgical service itself, from which the song must grow as the fruit grows from the tree." [3]

Full and Conscious Participation

"The Church, mother and teacher, brings us to express our faith through her rites, her prayers and chants. But just as the Word of God, in order to reach men, must borrow *men's language,* so faith and worship must express themselves *through*

---

[1] S. Mbunga, *Church Law and Bantu Music* (Schoneck, 1963), p. xiv.
[2] *The Constitution on the Sacred Liturgy* (Glen Rock, N.J.: Paulist Press, 1965), Art. 118.
[3] J. Gelineau, "Problems of Sacred Chant in the Missions," in *Teaching All Nations,* Vol. II, n. 1 (Hong Kong, 1965), p. 116; cf. *The Constitution on the Sacred Liturgy,* Art. 14.

the human culture of the faithful. Singing will have meaning in a person's life of faith only when it is expressed in his own words, rhythms and tunes." [4] Hence:

1. *As regards language: Kiswahili,* the Tanzanian national language, *should be the official liturgical language next to Latin.* Tribal languages should be discouraged in liturgy not only because of the nation's growth, integrity and unity but also because every Tanzanian is culturally disposed to understand Kiswahili or at least to learn it easily, either in primary schools or adult education projects. Where still necessary, tribal languages should be used for homilies and paraliturgical celebrations where only one tribe takes part. Those few dioceses that consider the tribal language obligatory for the fuller participation of their faithful in the liturgy would achieve the same effect if they worked to foster the national language among their flock.

2. *As regards rhythms and melodies:* the more African these are, the fuller will be the conscious participation. This statement is simply the application of Article 119 of the Constitution on the Sacred Liturgy which acknowledges the deep significance of the indigenous musical traditions of the peoples in the mission-lands in relation to their attempts *to adapt worship to their native genius.* Music throughout Africa is distinguished by the characteristic love of establishing *a tension between rhythms.* Pius X, writing on Sacred Music,[5] stated that its "principal function is *to clothe with an appropriate melody* the liturgical text which is proposed *to the understanding of the faithful:* its specific purpose is to give an increased efficacy to the text itself". If all this is true, where can this be better accomplished than through one's indigenous rhythms and melodies? If the mind is attuned to the words,[6] the faithful will be moved and led as fully as possible into the mystery. "If liturgical singing is borrowed

[4] J. Gelineau, "Renewal of Liturgical Singing in Mission Countries," in *Teaching All Nations,* Vol. I, n. 2 (1964), p. 233.

[5] Pius X, *Motu Proprio,* "Tra le sollecitudini" (Nov. 22, 1903) (*de instauratione musicae sacrae*).

[6] *Regula Monasteriorum,* Ch. 19: "Mens nostra concordet voci nostrae."

and foreign to the faithful in its verbal or rhythmic or melodic forms, it will remain a mere garment of faith without becoming part of its structure." [7]

3. This is true also *as regards the use of African musical instruments*. This question seems perhaps the most controversial problem, and a great many of us look at it with skepticism. But Vatican Council II thinks positively: ". . . other instruments [besides the pipe organ] also *may be admitted for use in divine worship, with the knowledge and consent of the competent territorial authority* . . . on condition that the instruments are suitable, or can be made suitable, for sacred use. . . ." [8] Experience has proved that even the drum falls under this category and can be made suitable for sacred use. If a drumbeat suitable for Christian chant is devised, it will be possible to integrate the accompaniment into the form proper to the holiness of the liturgy. At the meeting of African church music composers in Kitwe,[9] the use of drums in church was discussed in a special way, the results being the following: "The musicians held that *a new style of drumming* should be used for Christian worship. . . . It was also suggested that drumming in church *should be introduced slowly* and only at centers that showed themselves ready for it. . . . Rhythms borrowed from other areas, with which Christian congregations were not familiar, would therefore be especially suited for use in church."

4. *A New Swahili "Ordinarium Missae"*: Permitted to promote experimentation in African adaptation by the Constitution on the Sacred Liturgy,[10] the Tanganyika Episcopal Conference[11] instructed the Pastoral Institute of Bukumbi to authorize the National Liturgical Committee, as well as others (preferably co-opted members) working through their own initiative, to experiment and devise tunes and simple chants for those parts

[7] J. Gelineau, "Renewal of Liturgical Singing in Mission Countries," in *Teaching All Nations* (1964), p. 234.
[8] *The Constitution on the Sacred Liturgy*, Art. 120.
[9] Moto, Zambia (Feb. 1965), p. 7.
[10] Cf. *The Constitution on the Sacred Liturgy*, Arts. 40, 44 and 123.
[11] Tanganyika Episcopal Conference 33/64 (Rome, Oct. 28, 1964), Minute 10.

of the liturgy sung in the vernacular. Through the cooperation of three members of the Liturgical Committee, together with several co-opted members, *eight Swahili Kyries have been prepared, taped and mimeographed at the Pastoral Institute, Bukumbi,* to disperse to all dioceses interested in experimenting. The chants conform to the solutions discussed above and the requirements of the Constitution on the Sacred Liturgy (n. 121). The dioceses were asked to send in their results and suggestions for improvement. Later this Committee hopes to issue this *Kyriale* or the *New Swahili "Ordinarium Missae"* for singing. All this can easily be introduced by the ordinary in his diocese, with the exception of the new melodies of the Swahili parts sung by the celebrant and ministers at Swahili High Mass. These melodies require a special approval of the Tanzania Episcopal Conference.[12] Until then we will still have to use the "Toni Communes Missae" with text.

5. *A New Swahili "Proprium de Tempore":* Experiments on the new *Proprium de Tempore* have already begun at St. Augustine's Senior Seminary, Peramiho, and at some places within the diocese of Peramiho. The Pastoral Institute is arranging to extend the experimenting outside the diocese as well. Satisfactory results so far have been achieved. Just as for the *Ordinary of the Mass, the responsorial form,* which is the universal musical element in Africa, is used so that the whole congregation may easily sing even without a book. The cantors sing the psalm or corresponding text as given in the missal and *the congregation answers in a refrain* that is a central theme suitable for the particular liturgical period. Both for the *Ordinary* and the *Proper,* recorded tapes and musical notes are available from the Bukumbi Pastoral Institute.

Music for Active Participation

"Mother Church earnestly desires that all the faithful should be led to that full, conscious and active participation in liturgical

---

[12] *Instr. ad executionem Const. de Sacra Liturgia recte ordinandam* (Rome, Sept. 26, 1964), n. 42.

celebrations." [13] There can be the latter without the former, but the former helps the latter greatly, for one can sing actively without understanding fully what one sings.

For this purpose *any other music besides the pure African* can serve, provided that in the general opinion it is good, easy, simple and appealing. Such music transcends culture and language blockades in God's service and may serve as a common "denominatorial" ground where various musical cultures meet, given that all mankind has the same human nature. Such music can be found among *some Gregorian Chant pieces, simple foreign hymns and even among mixed styles.* Hence we need neither to simply discard all Church hymns brought by missionaries nor indiscriminately to receive more foreign melodies, but we must select most carefully.

In other words, we need a new Tanzanian hymnbook comprised of popular African religious hymns and well-selected, simple, favorite foreign hymns from the books already in use today in Tanzania. In this way, non-Tanzanians who take part in our public divine worship will perhaps feel inclined to join in the singing according to their musical styles. But, above all, the greatest care must be taken in this selection in order to achieve the right fusion of cultures in conformity with ethnomusicological principles. We must be realistic and realize that green leaves plastered over dried-up bark will not make a living tree.

What we have attempted in this article has been only to open a small window into the vast complexity of our Tanzanian church music. The task therein is immense and will not be accomplished in one generation. "It takes generations of creative artists to set a style which may be distinguished as characteristic of a people. Taste in music, as in other arts, is not the free choice of individuals but is conditioned by their inherited preferences, however much they may be modified or entrenched within a lifetime." [14]

[13] *The Constitution on the Sacred Liturgy,* Art. 14.
[14] TNR (Sept. 1964), p. 216.

But all their efforts will be paralyzed if there is no *cooperation between missionaries and the indigenous composers.* Africa is going through a period of profound cultural change at the moment, and it is important not to regard this process as a mere reshuffling of old African ideas with new Western ones. "There is a considerable chance that positive elements from the old cultures will exercise an important influence on the new situation." [15] When a new religion comes into contact with an old culture, "it changes it and is changed by it".[16] Hence, let us cast away all prejudices and selfish motives by a *profound supernatural Christian love* in which we exchange views freely, without forcing our opinions on others, and try to understand one another better. But one needs *broad-mindedness* to see that the present profound liturgical changes, humanly speaking, cannot be introduced without friction and that "missionary customs of several decades cannot easily be abolished" [17] except through selflessness, stoutheartedness, brotherly love and mutual understanding.[18]

[15] A.-E. M. Shorter, W. F., *AFER,* Vol. VII, n. 2 (April 1965), p. 167.

[16] C. Dawson, *Religion and Culture* (London, 1949), p. 61.

[17] *Pastoral Information T.E.C.,* DSM, n. 5 (1965), p. 1.

[18] Luigi Bertini, in *Welt Mission* (Vienna: May-August, 1964), pp. 20-21.

✠ Wilhelmus van Bekkum, S.V.D./*Ruteng, Indonesia*

Liturgical Development in Indonesia

The Editor* of the CONCILIUM volume on the liturgy, in attempting to get a comprehensive survey of the Indonesian liturgy, found his task rather difficult. Most Rev. W. van Bekkum, S.V.D., Bishop of the diocese of Ruteng on the island of Flores, launched the survey out of his great concern for the Indonesian liturgy. The country is as large as Europe and communications between the numerous islands are difficult, a situation that discourages frequent contact and effective cooperation. The missionaries continue to labor at their remote posts, trying to give a new shape to the liturgy with experiments of their own, but have no opportunity to discuss these experiments with each other. Bishop van Bekkum organized a three-day liturgical conference in August, 1965, and was able to obtain a general picture of the various situations. During this conference, held in the Cistercian Priory of Middle Java, a solemn high Mass was celebrated in the Indonesian language, and was widely welcomed. The conference showed that on the various islands (such as Timor, Flores, Celebes, Java, Sumatra, Borneo, etc.) musical texts were in use, edited and published by the missionaries themselves. One published a book with Indonesian texts set to Gregorian melodies, another used Indonesian music by native composers, and another strove to modernize gamelan music for liturgical purposes.

* This article was written by the editorial board from notes supplied by Bishop van Bekkum.

It is impossible to give a scientific survey of the situation in Indonesia, and certainly for the whole of East Asia, because the lack of communication and the heterogeneous character of the reports make it extremely difficult to collect and check the material. On the other hand, the reader might find it useful to know what is happening in some places. Here, then, are two reports as they were sent in. They indicate in detail what is being done in one parish, and on a particular island.

I

THE PROJECT FOR A LITURGICAL CELEBRATION IN THE PARISH OF MANO[1]

1. *What Has Already Been Achieved*

(a) The *Ordinary of the Mass,* with the liturgical text itself in Manggarai (by special privilege). Mass no. 32 from the Dére Manggarai is not very satisfactory, first because the same melody is used for all parts of the Mass, and fails to convey the difference in character between one part and another (*Kyrie, Sanctus,* etc.). Second, there is no distinction between the *Ordinary* and the *Proper of the Mass:* thus the *Introit, Kyrie, Gloria, Gradual, Credo, Offertory,* etc., are all sung with the same melody. This obscures the structure of the Mass. Third, the text is very poor, and too much depends upon the inventiveness of the composer with too little account taken of the text of the liturgy and Scripture. Fourth, since the Mass serves all purposes, it is never connected with a particular phase of the liturgical year.

This criticism of Mass no. 32 shows the direction in which we want to work.

(b) Another *Ordinary of the Mass,* in which each part has its own melody, is taken respectively from Sanda manga, Tura-

---

[1] The report on this parish comes from the parish priest, N. van der Molen.

latung and Pakikaba.[2] Such a choice of melody creates an atmosphere that corresponds with that of the liturgical contents. This has already been printed in quantity. Musical notation is omitted purposely because experience has taught us that when people sing from notes, each sings differently; there is, therefore, little uniformity of liturgical singing in Manggarai. We have found it preferable to send an instructor to the various groups.

(c) For the *Proper of the Mass* that changes with the liturgical seasons, we take the text of the *Antiphona ad Introitum* (as it has been called since the pre-conciliar Holy Week changes) as *"walé"*,[3] to be sung by the people, and a psalm as *"tjako"*,[4] after each verse of which the people answer with the *"walé"*. For every liturgical season we have a different melody for the psalm of the *Introit* and the *"walé"*, and the words of the *"walé"* vary for each Mass according to the antiphon of the Mass. We always have a translation of this antiphon which we can use as a whole or in part, and which is easy to practice before each Mass. This applies to *Easter, Pentecost, Corpus Christi*, for the Mass *Terribilis est* and for the ordinary Sundays after Pentecost. The texts are not yet ready for all Masses, but they are being prepared for every Sunday of the year. For the time being the melody for the *Gradual, Offertory* and *Communion* remains the same insofar as the text is concerned.

2. *What Is Still to Be Accomplished*

(a) We must find an appropriate melody for the *whole Proper of the Mass, i.e.,* for the *Introit, Gradual, Offertory* and *Communion*, according to the liturgical year.

(b) When this is done we must begin with melodies for each individual Mass, *e.g.,* for *Ash Wednesday*, for the first Sunday of *Lent*, for *Passion Sunday*, and so on. This will take years, but the work will be carried on quietly and steadily.

[2] These are religious songs of the pagans
[3] Response or refrain.
[4] Leading a song.

II

A BRIEF SURVEY OF THE NEW LITURGICAL CHANT IN THE "DAWAN"
VERNACULAR ON THE ISLAND OF TIMOR[5]

This brief report on the island of Timor (diocese of Atambua)
is limited to one of the three dialects spoken on Timor. This is
the Dawan language which is used by some 500,000 people.
The two other dialects of Timor are Belu and Marai. For the
Belu dialect we have a printed songbook, called *Dakado*, published by Pertjetakan Arnoldus at the end of 1961. It contains
no native melodies; they are simply translations from the *Jubilate*
with European melodies in the old style of the 19th century.

The situation is somewhat better, though not yet ideal, in the
case of the Dawan language. Here we have a songbook called
Tsi tanaeb Uis Neno by Father Vinzent Lechovic, S.V.D.,
published by Pertjetakan Arnoldus, Ende Flores. The first edition
of 3,000 copies appeared in 1957; the second followed in 1962
with 11,000 copies. What are the origins of this little book?

The official language of Timor is Indonesian. Many Christians
learned this language at school, and so they used Indonesian
songs from the book *Jubilate*. But there was also a large group
of Christians who had not been to school. What could they sing
in church? They were also taught the Indonesian songs, but this
was a foreign language, little used in the villages. Even the school
children practically forget it after spending some years in their
villages.

We had small groups of school children everywhere who sang
during the Mass, but the adults took no part. In the regions of
the diaspora the situation was worse because the Protestants for
some time had already possessed their own Dawan songbook,
called *Si knino oenoe ma moeni* (P. Middelkoop [The Hague:
J. V. Voorhoeve, 1941]). It contained songs with European
melodies such as were in use in the Netherlands, but the people

---

[5] This report comes from Father V. Lechovic, S.V.D., who lives in
Timor.

understood the contents and took a lively part in the singing. Our Christians could only pray, and here and there take part in Indonesian singing. Several missionaries, among them Father van Wissing and Msgr. van de Tillaart, tried to work out a text in Dawan to be sung to the known melodies. It is this need that prompted the songbook, *Tsi tanaeb Uis Neno,* with foreign European melodies that the people remembered from school. Italian, German and Slovak melodies were also incorporated, some with great success. Then came some experimenting with indigenous songs from Flores and Timor. People could buy these booklets cheaply, and the adults among them enjoyed singing known melodies in their own language. This produced a wave of enthusiasm for singing in church among the people.

But together with this modest success, we found that difficulties arose from songs with a text that changed with every stanza. Our people must often sing in dark chapels, frequently without light or assisted only by small lamps. It was difficult to learn all the stanzas by heart. We needed another form of songs, so we enriched the second edition of the songbook with new material. We chose the responsorial form as the most suitable; here the people have only to learn a short refrain.

Apart from this we chose pentatonic melodies as almost all indigenous melodies are based on the five-tone scale. Thus we introduced music for the Mass that was new both in form and in melody. For the *Proper* we used psalm-singing with a refrain. This psalmody was either a Latin choral work, or free and new. One should remember that so far we do not have a complete translation of the psalms. The composer of the psalmody used at Mass must provide both the melody and the translation. The melodies are composed on the basis of the five-tone scale; it was impossible to take over popular melodies as they existed because in the Dawan language there are no serious religious songs. Instead, we took over the form and structure of their songs and proceeded by way of variations-on-a-theme. Thus the original melody was concealed but people found the "new" melody rather familiar and easy to sing. These melodies were quickly learned; when the text was translated into Indonesian the new melodies could also be used outside this region.

In the *Ordinary of the Mass,* the *Kyrie* is sung in the five-tone scale. The eighth Mass (*Missa de Angelis*) with the text in Dawan is very popular. The *Gloria* proved too long, so we turned it into a song with refrain. We did the same with the *Credo,* of which we use the shorter form, the *Apostles' Creed.* The choir sings each article as a recitative and the people answer "Amen" after each. It was a practical solution to make this difficult piece short and easy to sing. The *Sanctus* is also sung with the help of a refrain. It was often noticed that since the refrain becomes tiresome when too short, a certain length must be observed.

Here we must mention the Negro Spirituals, many of which are pentatonic with a refrain. We introduced some of these melodies successfully, *e.g.,* the song, "Swing Low, Sweet Chariot". Since our diocese enjoys the privilege of the German solemn Mass, we use some text formulas with paraphrases, *e.g.,* an *Advent Mass,* a *Lenten Mass,* a *Requiem Mass* and a formula for a *Mass of Our Lady.*

Most singing in our churches and chapels is done without a harmonium, and the organ is not yet known on Timor. Indigenous instruments comprise a violin, a sort of guitar and flutes. Apart from these they use percussion instruments, the drum and the gong. These percussion instruments can be used to accompany pentatonic melodies, but on the whole the time is not yet ripe for this. Here and there modern instruments are tried—the double-bass, the guitar and the accordion—to create a more lively mood, but this does not lead to active participation by the people. It sounds like a theatrical performance with a sentimental slant; this is no solution to enriching the liturgical celebration.

What in the final analysis are our difficulties? First, we need indigenous talent great enough to deal creatively and scientifically with the problem. Sometimes prejudice makes people cling to a foreign culture, a foreign language and a foreign music. The aim of our reform remains, nevertheless, to look for treasures of indigenous culture and to use these in the Church's worship. One must begin with collecting indigenous music, a labor that still awaits an explorer. Then there is the problem of the one language. Indonesian is used everywhere although culture varies widely from one island to another. We must find out what songs and what kind of religious music can be introduced everywhere. The first approaches to indigenous liturgical singing have already been discovered. We must look for further possibilities in this direction, above all by closer collaboration between the neighboring islands.

✠ Guilford C. Young/*Hobart, Australia*

Church Music in Australia

Immediately after the proclamation
of the Constitution on the Sacred
Liturgy by Pope Paul VI, the
Australian Episcopal Conference directed its Episcopal Committee on the Liturgy to take the necessary steps to prepare
texts for the adoption of English in those parts of the liturgy
where it was considered necessary. The most urgent need was for
Mass texts. Certain missals in common usage were accepted to
provide the variable parts of the Mass, but for the parts of the
Ordinary in which the congregation participated, *i.e.*, the *Responses, Kyrie, Gloria,* etc., a uniform translation was adopted
for Australia. This had been prepared by literary and musical
experts to insure that the text not only was theologically accurate
and expressed in good English prose but also that it was suitable
to be both sung and spoken by a congregation. Certain traditional
translations were changed precisely because they could not easily
be sung or recited by a large group of people. This task was
accomplished more quickly in Australia than in most other
countries because of the thinking and experimenting in such
adaptation problems that had begun several years before when
the pre-conciliar requests of bishops and discussions clearly
indicated that some form of vernacular liturgy would emerge
from the Council.

To insure a certain basic unity of sung texts throughout Australia, the bishops were invited to nominate music experts for the purpose of submitting such music for liturgical texts to the bishops. A music sub-committee was set up consisting of five priests and two laymen, all practicing church musicians from various parts of Australia. To these was added a priest expert in Scripture, the Rev. Denis Murphy, M.S.C.

The members of the committee were: Rev. Percy Jones, Mus. Doc. Sac., Chairman (Melbourne), Rev. Albert Lynch (Perth), Rev. Joseph Howe (Tasmania), Rev. Ronald Harden (Sydney), Rev. D. G. Briglia (Melbourne), Mr. J. Govenlock (Adelaide), and Mr. R. Connolly (Sydney).

The task of this committee was twofold: (1) to prepare official chants in the vernacular, based whenever possible on the traditional simple plainsong melodies for all sung parts of the liturgy which would be officially authorized by the Episcopal Conference for use throughout Australia; (2) to examine and recommend to the bishops for their approval other music by contemporary composers or adaptations of the vernacular to other musical compositions which could be sung in the strictly liturgical rites.

Despite the long distances separating the members, this committee met a number of times. Working on drafts prepared by the Chairman, it was soon able to submit to the Episcopal Liturgy Committee sufficient music to begin sung Masses by the end of March, 1965, just two weeks after the Instruction for the Implementation of the Constitution. As a result, the following publications are now available for liturgical use in Australia:

1. *Officially Authorized by the Bishops*

(a) An insert for altar missals, containing chants for *Prayers, Readings, Acclamations and Responses,* the *Lord's Prayer and embolism,* and intonations of the *Gloria* and *Credo.*

(b) A plainsong hymnal, containing two plainsong Masses (*Kyrie, Gloria,* etc.) as well as *Asperges,* the *Prayer of the Faithful,* the *Lord's Prayer* and all *Acclamations and Responses.* It also contains chants for benediction of the blessed sacrament, confirmation, episcopal receptions, Marian antiphons and the *Te Deum*.

(c) The texts for the sung *Proper* of all Masses for all the Sundays and first-class feasts throughout the year (2 vols.), especially translated (based on the Kleist-Lynam version of the Psalter) for singing to psalm-tones.

(d) A set of the eight traditional psalm-tone melodies, cadentially adapted for English, with a set of suitable Alleluia melodies for the eight modes.

(e) A Holy Week book for choirs, containing all the sung texts for the ceremonies from Passion Sunday to Easter Sunday.

(f) A Holy Week book for priests, containing the traditional chants (adapted to English) of the Passion according to St. Matthew and St. John, the Veneration of the Cross, the Bidding Prayers (Good Friday), the *Exsultet* and the Blessing of Baptismal Water (Easter Vigil).

(g) *In preparation:* the *Prefaces* of the Mass in English.

2. *Other Music Approved*

Four Masses by contemporary Australian composers, as well as some modern settings of the *Propers,* have already been approved, two of which have been published and widely used. This work of examining compositions submitted by composers continues. Although the committee wishes to encourage composers, it has set high standards, realizing that congregational music (although it must be within the capability of the people) must not be trite or of poor musical quality.

The main problem of vernacular church music is the lack of a suitable translation of the Bible, particularly of the psalms and canticles. If the choral and congregational recitation and singing of the *Introit, Gradual,* etc., is to become a dignified prayer and not a confused babel of voices, these texts must have a rhythm to allow such common recitation or singing. None of the present accepted translations in common use have this necessary quality. The Kleist translation was chosen because it is written in iambic prose. In addition, it is extremely accurate as a translation, but it also has its defects.

What is needed more urgently than anything else is a translation by true poets, assisted or advised by musicians who can indicate what is and what is not singable, and by actors who know what are the limitations of the spoken word and what can be grasped by listening rather than by hearing. This is not a problem peculiar to Australia or to the English language; it is perhaps the chief universal problem in the use of any vernacular in the liturgy.

* All officially authorized publications listed above are available from the Advocate Press, a'Beckett St., Melbourne, C. 1. Australia.

Two modern Masses as well as those listed under 1 (b) and 1 (d) are available from the publishers: Allan's Music Pty. Ltd., Collins Street, Melbourne. Companion editions of 1 (b) and 1 (d) are published by Allan's Music Pty. Ltd. A companion to the Holy Week choir book 1 (e) is published by the Advocate Press.

Two L.P. recordings are available from the Catholic Radio and Television Office, a'Beckett Street, Melbourne. One contains the two plainsong Masses and other material in the authorized plainsong hymnal 1 (b), sung by St. Patrick's Cathedral Choir. The second is a demonstration record of most of the Holy Week music for both celebrant and choir 1 (d) and (f) sung by the Rev. Percy Jones, Chairman of the Music Sub-committee. These records have made the task of choirs and choirmasters throughout Australia much easier and have helped to maintain uniformity of performance.

PART III

DOCUMENTATION

CONCILIUM

*Office of the Executive Secretary
Nijmegen, Netherlands*

The liturgy is undergoing a kind of decentralization. An adaptation to the different nations, languages and cultures is perceptible. It is now thought that this variety will bring more life into the liturgy of each nation. On the other hand, the Constitution on the Sacred Liturgy is determined to guide this pluriformity along the right road. Thus, a frame of reference has been given so that from many forms a real uniformity will result.

With this explanation, the following articles allow us to draw some conclusions as to how far, in the last two years, the Constitution has been put into practice. Two outstanding tendencies—pluriformity, uniformity—claim our attention. The degree will vary from one country to another.

Paul Brunner, S.J./*Manila, Philippines*

Liturgical Renewal in Asia: Achievements and Hopes

The active participation of the faithful in communal worship began on a truly large scale on March 7, 1965. From all corners reports told of enthusiastic welcome given to the changes, especially the introduction of the vernacular into Catholic liturgy. Communities, for years reluctant to assume an active role in community worship, responded unhesitatingly as soon as they were permitted to express themselves in their own language.

Translations

The multiplicity of problems involved in the work of translation absorbs much energy and attention, but despite this, every episcopal conference in Asia has, quite significantly, urged Rome to allow them as much vernacular in the liturgy as possible. Even in countries which have the advantage of a single national language, like Vietnam and Thailand, prescinding for the moment some dialects of aborigines, the translation problems involved are more complicated than those in Latin or Anglo-Saxon languages.

Japan offers an example of such problems. The Japanese use different styles in conversation depending on the personages involved. When one speaks to a superior, the exalted style or "bungôtai" is used; when one speaks to peers, the simple style or "kôgôtai" is employed. The translators decided to use the exalted style when the words are addressed to God (as in the *Gloria, Sanctus, Credo,* etc.); the simple style is employed in the dialogues between the priest and the faithful. This mixture of styles, which sometimes occurs in the same prayer, is distasteful to some and the translators have not been spared criticisms.

The Chinese translators, too, faced a very difficult task. Their text is destined for use in Taiwan, Macau, Hong Kong and in the Chinese diaspora (*i.e.,* in all of Asia) where, in addition to the national language, there are four main dialects: Cantonese, Shanghaiese, Hacca and Amoy. The written characters for all these dialects are the same, although spelling, vocabulary and syntax differ. Consequently, common expressions for all these Chinese dialects must be found, although in keeping with the various dialects, these expressions which are written alike are spelled differently.

Fortunately, the more elegant style used in newspapers and books provides a common denominator, but the translators must always strive to maintain a simplicity to make the text understandable to those who lack a higher education. Such a solution permits Christians of different linguistic backgrounds (often grouped together in the same parish) to recite the same text, each with his own pronunciation.

Elsewhere, the problem is still more acute. In Malaysia, besides the Chinese dialects, English, Tamil and Malay are spoken. In the Philippines, there are 66 dialects. From these, the Episcopal Conference has promoted 8 to the rank of liturgical languages together with Spanish which is rapidly disappearing, and English which is understood by 37 percent of the population. English is indeed the common linguistic vehicle of many Asian communities, a fact which facilitates the liturgical renewal a great deal. What is done overseas in the liturgical field can also be used here. Everywhere, regional commissions have been set up to make translations into the various dialects. Considerable variants are found even in the same linguistic area. Since translation is also a matter of taste, agreement is often reached with great difficulty. It also happens that some dioceses reject the translation made by the regional commission and make their own—a procedure not conducive to unity.

Adaptation

All Episcopal Conferences have shown the intention to gradually incorporate in the ritual liturgical symbols suited to the spirit and character of their countries. To this end they have entrusted their national commissions with the task of studying national customs, particularly with respect to the marriage rite. It is not surprising that, at this stage, little has been achieved in the matter of adaptation. The rituals used during these past few years in Japan, Taiwan and India, and the partial translations of the ritual made for Vietnam, Thailand, etc., are, as a whole, mere replicas of the Roman ritual. Before borrowing signs and symbols from their particular cultures, it is still more urgent that our clergy be imbued with the spirit of the Roman liturgy and take advantage of its pastoral potentialities if they wish to avoid mistakes that they shall later regret.

However, there are some examples which may give an idea of what the future liturgy in Asia will be like. As far as we know, Japan is the only country which has adopted changes in the ritual on a national scope. A profound bow has replaced the genuflection, and instead of kissing the Missal, the minister simply raises it to his forehead. Everywhere else, it seems, experiments have been confined to the limits of pilot stations from which they shall pass, once they have proved useful to the diocesan or national level. In Vietnam, the Benedictines near Hue have modified Mass vestments after the style of mandarin robes and have adopted the large ceremonial hat. The use of the mandarin robes and hat has been tagged as archaic and it could well be asked if such a return to past forms might not risk creating for the Church an image of outdatedness.

In Java, the "gamelan", a musical instrument, is used in the three processions in the Mass and accompanies the people when they sing. The recitative tone for the readings and prayers is likewise borrowed from Javanese tradition. The gong replaces the bell at the Consecration. During the Canon, a parasol (called a "songsong"), used to honor men of high rank, is held above the celebrant to emphasize the real presence of Christ on the altar. The parasol accompanies the priest while he distributes holy communion. An Offertory procession solemnly carries to the altar the offerings of the faithful and all that is needed for the celebration of the sacrifice.

In the diocese of Raighahr-Ambikapur (India), we note a beautiful custom that links daily life with Sunday Mass. "Each day before cooking the rice, the mother of the family, together with her children, puts aside a portion of rice called 'God's share'. A brief ceremony accompanies this gesture. After making the sign of the cross, everyone kneels down and the mother says this prayer: 'Heavenly Father, as an offering to the Holy Sacrifice of the Mass, I put aside this portion of rice. Please look down upon us, the old and the young, and see our poverty.' All reply, 'Amen'. The following Sunday, the rice put aside by all the families is gathered together into great baskets, and at the Offertory the baskets are carried by two parish representatives up to the celebrant as a sign of the parish's participation in the sacrifice" (cf. E. R. Hambye, S.J., "Le Renouveau liturgique dans le monde, l'Inde," in *La Maison-Dieu* 74, p. 151).

Some adaptations obviously need to be made and one sometimes wonders why they are not done. For example, in the new Chinese baptismal ritual for women, it is surprising to see that the anointing of chest and shoulders is retained when one realizes the intense embarrassment of a Chinese woman when touched by a person of the opposite sex. Likewise, the bishops of Taiwan did not provide for the distribution of communion under both species in the marriage ceremony. This practice would be most meaningful in China since a cup of wine shared by the couple used to be part of the traditional Chinese marriage rite. This custom was observed by the first Chinese Christians, as is evident at the end of the prayer recited by the couple: "After the prayer, drink from the nuptial cup."

The limits of this article do not allow me to survey the efforts made in musical adaptation. However, I would like to mention the beautiful Indian pieces composed for the Eucharistic Congress in Bombay. Among them were the psalms in Tamil composed at the catechetical school in Tindiwanam. In the Philippines, a Mass, based on native melodies approximating Gregorian modes and adaptable to nearly all vernacular texts, was composed by the Benedictines of the Abbey of Our Lady of Montserrat in Manila.

Expectation

What we in Asia expect of the post-conciliar commission is the restoration of the teaching power and flexibility for adaptation possessed by the liturgy in its origins. Especially, the "proclamation of the death of Christ" (1 Cor. 11, 26), which reaches its climax in the Canon of the Mass, needs to be expressed in revised forms.

We explain to our faithful that the Canon is the great thanksgiving prayer that the "holy people" raise to God through the mediation of the celebrant and that this great prayer was once proclaimed in an understandable language by the priest together with "those standing about him" (circumstantes), just as Christ did in the Cenacle in the midst of His apostles. And then we urge the faithful to ratify this eucharistic prayer with a vigorous "Amen".

Unfortunately, our people do not find any application in the Church of what was explained to them in catechism class. At the Canon, the link which was forged between the priest and his flock during the liturgy of the Word weakens. They part again, so to speak, and take separate functions—the priest at the altar and the faithful in the nave. In fact, they do not know exactly what they are supposed to do. The Canon becomes a kind of interlude between the *Sanctus* and the *Pater Noster*, during which old people cough, children cry, and the whole congregation grows restless in the unbearable heat.

It is the missionaries' ardent wish that the post-conciliar commission restore the Canon to its throbbing significance as the great oblation of God's people in the New Covenant.

✠ Guilford C. Young/*Hobart, Australia*

Liturgy in Australia

R eform of the liturgy in Australia was licensed by decisions made by the Conference of the Bishops of Australia at meetings in Sydney in March and June of 1964 and their subsequent ratification by the *Consilium ad Exsequendam Constitutionem de Sacra Liturgia* (Commission for the Implementation of the Constitution on the Sacred Liturgy).

Since that time the *Ritus Servandus in Celebratione Missae* of the Sacred Congregation of Rites (January 27, 1965) has been adopted and other modifications have been made in light of experience following consultation with the *Consilium*. The Australian hierarchy voted for widest possible use of the vernacular.

All parts of the Mass that are said aloud are in English, including the *Preface,* but not *"Nobis quoque peccatoribus",* the *"Per Ipsum",* or the celebrant's *"Domine, non sum dignus".* Translation and selection of texts were made by the Australian hierarchy's liturgy committee.

Members of the committee are Archbishop Justin D. Simonds of Melbourne (president), Archbishop Guilford C. Young of Hobart, Bishop Brian Gallagher of Port Pirie, Bishop Thomas V. Cahill of Cairns (secretary), Bishop Launcelot J. Goody of Bunbury, and Auxiliary Bishop John Cullinane of Canberra and

Goulburn. Their translation of the *Ordinary of the Mass* was marked by a departure from stylized hieratic forms of expression and special attention was given to the demands of English as spoken by a large body of people.

Three commonly used English-language missals were approved for the *Proper* and *Common*. A fourth choice was given when the Australian hierarchy adopted the Canadian English-language missal.

All other eucharistic rites—such as benediction of the blessed sacrament and communion for the sick—are entirely in English. Rites for six sacraments are completely in English, only holy orders being excepted. Translations for the sacraments are those contained in the old *Baltimore Ritual,* the later United States' *Collectio Rituum,* and *The Small Ritual* of the British hierarchy.

Allocutions of ordination rites are in English, as are the litanies, the *Ordinary, Proper, Common,* etc., but the sacramental formulas remain in Latin. Rites for the sacramentals—including funerals—are also in English.

The Liturgical Press (Collegeville, Minn.) translation of the divine office has been approved and is widely used in Australia. Use of English has been accompanied by new emphases that delineate more clearly the structure of liturgical rites. This has been most successful in the Mass, where there is now a clear line of demarcation between the Celebration of the Word and the Celebration of the Eucharist. It was achieved, as in other parts of the world, by conducting the Service of the Word away from the altar. The priest's early presidential role is being recognized. The now familiar sight of the Bible in many churches is conveying the sense of its fundamental importance and the eucharistic significance of the altar is presenting itself more clearly. Congregations are beginning to see themselves as "a people of the chalice and the book".

The division of the rites has been accompanied by a division of the roles in worship. Congregations respond wholeheartedly and in many cases have completely taken over the *Kyrie, Gloria, Credo* and *Agnus Dei.* Choirs and whole-congregation singing are slowly making their way into the liturgy. In some places the *Introit, Gradual,* etc., are recited by the whole congregation; in other places these are read by small *schola* groups. Laymen read the Scripture lessons not taken from the gospels.

This description of the liturgy must be qualified by pointing out that decisions made by the Australian hierarchy are not binding on individual dioceses. Implementation of decisions is at various stages in the 25 Sees of Australia. Although legislation allows for sweeping liturgical reform, in practice there is wide variation. However, most dioceses have already reached or are approaching the level of involvement outlined above.

It can be claimed that the vast majority of Australian Catholics and their pastors are very pleased with the liturgical renewal. Articulate opposition has been slight, mostly centering on the texts used in the new rites. In-depth criticism in these early stages has not been of the nature necessary to purify and enrich the liturgy of the Australian Church. At the present time three major challenges face the liturgical movement in Australia that are concerned with overcoming deficiencies in the pattern of faith as practiced in the past.

First of all, Australian Catholics do not have a tradition of devotion to the Bible, which has been regarded as more or less the domain of Protestantism.

Secondly, the new liturgy is not able to draw on a heritage of hymns. It is doubtful if the average Australian Catholic would know as many as five hymns—and most likely they would be of a mood not in harmony with the liturgical revival.

And thirdly, although on a person-to-person basis Australian priests have a record of pastoral achievement few countries could match, Australia is not accustomed to good preaching either as to content or style, possibly because of the demands of such exacting service.

But under the influence of Vatican Council II and in the atmosphere of freedom and initiative it has engendered, the massive program of remedying these defects has commenced. Dioceses have started campaigns to establish a pastoral liturgy;

hymns are being composed to meet theological, esthetic and popular demands; study groups and seminars on the liturgy and the Bible are multiplying. The reform has spread over the breadth of the continent and has changed every facet of the liturgy. The major task of the Church in Australia is to give depth and richness to this experience.

Bonifatius Luykx, O.Praem./*Leopoldville, Rep. of Congo*

The Liturgical Renewal in Africa

Outsiders were surprised at the energetic role of the African bishops in the debate on the Constitution on the Sacred Liturgy. For us Africans, this "active participation" was simply what we had expected, because in Africa the liturgy plays a relatively far more important role than in the old Christian countries where a deeply rooted individualism obstructs the communal expression of man's relation to God, both among the clergy and the laity. This is the first point we must keep in mind in discussing the liturgical situation in Africa (and here I speak mainly for Africa south of the equator).

1. It is good for a Westerner to realize once and for all that the African is, by nature, deeply religious. This means first of all that he has an intrinsically religious attitude toward reality. In an astonishingly natural way he lives more in the invisible world than in the visible one. The invisible is more real to him; he is vitally concerned with it, and it is through worship that he is in contact with it. That is why he is so easily moved by the symbol of the liturgy, which is the foundation of worship. Secondly, he has an irresistible need *to express* his religious experiences through the whole gamut of human activities, from dance to prayer. And he does all this communally, because the community is not something alien to him; rather, it is himself, multiplied and expanded. He needs the others. He cannot exist alone, and so he cannot meet God alone.

2. For these two reasons the whole problem of the liturgy is very different in Africa from that in the West, as will become clearer later on. In Africa we build on a preexisting situation that is infinitely more favorable than elsewhere. This explains why, all along the line, the renewal of the liturgy has fallen on fertile soil. The reports that have come in from various African countries show that both the missionaries and the indigenous clergy have put liturgical innovations into practice to the best of their ability, as if they were obvious and had long been expected.

In many regions and for the greater number of Christians, the liturgical celebration is, in fact, *the sole means of catechizing* or of continued evangelization. Therefore, every missionary wishes the liturgy to recover its full power of sanctification and instruction so that the faithful can take part as actively as possible and draw all the potential profit from it.[1] This also explains why the liturgical renewal goes hand in hand with the renewal of instruction, started a few years earlier, when the need for sounder catechetics had been recognized.

3. On the other hand, apart from these consolations, there are also some discouraging elements. First of all, both clergy and laity badly need liturgical formation. One may even say that on this point more than on any other we are confronted with an "underdeveloped territory". If, in spite of this lack of formation (there are, of course, exceptions), so much has nevertheless been achieved, it has been due mainly to the outstanding zeal of the missionaries and the innate liturgical sense of the native clergy. The *first problem,* therefore, is that of *bringing about a liturgical formation.*

According to the demands of the Constitution on the Sacred Liturgy (Arts. 16ff.), we shall need to make an exceptional effort in this field, primarily in our own missionary schools. Most missionaries belong to modern congregations where they receive little in the way of a liturgical spirit, but they generally welcome

[1] *The Constitution on the Sacred Liturgy* (Glen Rock, N.J.: Paulist Press, 1965), Arts. 31ff.; see my paper given at Katigondo in the *Revue du Clergé Africain* (November, 1964).

the renewal taking place in the Church. This openness is particularly noticeable in the younger generation of missionaries, although more so in the French-speaking countries of Africa than in the English-speaking ones. The English quite clearly suffer from the liturgical backwardness of the English-speaking mother countries (although in other respects they are usually more advanced than the French).

There is also still a great deal of backwardness in the houses where the native clergy are trained. Henceforth, liturgy will have to be one of the principal subjects, on a level with dogma, moral theology, scripture and canon law. It must be taught by a fully qualified professor, as required by the Constitution on the Sacred Liturgy (Art. 16) and as particularly emphasized by the pope after the second session of the Council. But we may have to show still more patience, since the whole question of the seminaries needs a fresh basic approach. Specialized institutions in Europe have already done much in this field for Africa.

In this regard I must first mention *Lumen Vitae* in Brussels. It is true that this institution concentrates primarily on catechetical formation, but this is indirectly reflected in liturgical training. Credit should also be given to the liturgical school of the Abbey of St. Andrew in Bruges which from the beginning has attracted many African students, mostly priests. A number of Africans and missionaries for Africa have taken courses at the liturgical institutes of Paris and at the University of Notre Dame in the United States. Occasionally, however, this formation in "white" institutions has disadvantages in that some too zealous disciples injudiciously adopt the customs and opinions of their Western masters or schools only to find that they cannot be applied: there is a slight difference between Saint-Séverin and Africa.

For the training of the older missionaries, a number of liturgical days of study have been organized in the various mother countries. The effort of the Fathers of Scheut in this regard is particularly noteworthy: all of their missionaries who are on leave in Europe must regularly attend the conferences held especially for them which are given by specialists in that field. In this way they receive a brief "aggiornamento" and are inserted into the movement of the liturgical renewal.

4. Much has already been done for the formation of clergy and laity in the mission countries themselves. Special mention must be made of the Pan-African Congress on Liturgy and Catechetics (August 29-September 4, 1964) in Katigondo (Uganda). It was arranged by the indefatigable Fr. J. Hofinger, S.J., who had previously organized in 1959 the well-known Congress on Liturgy and the Missions in Uden-Nijmegen. The 1964 Congress is best understood as an expansion of the one in Nijmegen. The African Cardinal Rugambwa presided and Archbishop Hurley of Durban led most of the discussions. There were representatives from all the countries of southern Africa as well as some foreign experts and observers. The spirit was excellent and much was achieved; but here, too, the difference between the French-speaking and the English-speaking countries was obvious: the former were far ahead of the latter, for the reasons mentioned above. Anyone interested in the liturgical and catechetical situation of Africa should read the report of this Congress.[2] It is a pity that not much has as yet been done in practice to implement the resolutions adopted at Katigondo. Africa moves slowly; it has too many irons in the fire, but the foundation has been laid on which we can continue to build.

5. In all this work in regard to the liturgical renewal, much credit should be given to the specialist centers set up in Africa itself. Originally these centers started with a few people (*e.g.,* a bishop and an assistant, or a professor of a seminary with his colleagues, as was the case in the catechetical center of Mayidi, Congo). Recently a few centers have been set up with *experts released from other work,* who handle the matter more methodically, as at Usumbura in Ruanda (the White Fathers) and the Center of Pastoral Studies in Leopoldville, Congo (Missionaries of Scheut).

[2] The English text has been published in the periodical *Teaching All Nations* (Manila, 1964); the French text (but only the main papers and resolutions) in *Revue du Clergé Africain* (November, 1964).

Since the hierarchy of the Congo has adopted this last center as its own, it can work more effectively throughout that territory. This favorable situation might well serve as an example for other countries. The person in charge of liturgy at this center gives liturgical retreats everywhere and leads days of study attended by a large part of the clergy and often by the leading members of the teaching profession. By encouraging composers and sending them model texts for various compositions, he hopes to collect, within a short period of time, a reasonably extensive repertoire of decent liturgical compositions in the principal languages. These are published by the Center in the form of handy song-cards. The periodical *Orientations Pastorales,* to which all priests and institutes subscribe *ex officio,* informs readers of the most important liturgical events; texts are suggested for not strictly liturgical services; practical directives are given for the best ways of living the liturgy in the special circumstances of the mission; the best books are reviewed, etc. In the meantime, the person in charge of Scripture has the responsibility of providing good translations and editions of the Bible. The Center also publishes an inexpensive popular missal and ritual. In short, it is clear that such a center, composed of experts and priests who are released from other duties, can provide an outstanding service.

I have already referred to the part played by the periodicals. It is of course impossible to mention more than the best known ones. First of all, there is the veteran *Revue du Clergé Africain* (Seminary of Mayidi); this periodical published some remarkable studies in recent years. The *Orientations Pastorales* of Leopoldville has previously been described. *Jeunes Eglises* (Bruges) is particularly valuable because of its frequent publication of studies contributed by the African students of the Liturgical Institute of St. Andrew's Abbey. The widest circulation in the English-speaking countries is enjoyed by the *African Ecclesiastical Review* (Masaka, Uganda), which regularly contains excellent studies of liturgical problems. *Vivante Afrique,* on the other hand, is an illustrated journal (of very high quality), but even so it has already devoted several issues to topics immediately related to our theme, such as the splendid issue on Ethiopia, the Eastern Liturgies, and others.

6. The introduction of the Constitution on the Sacred Liturgy and the Instruction of September 26, 1964, which took place on March 7, 1965, led to more intense liturgical activity. Diocesan liturgical commissions were set up practically everywhere and instructed to implement this official introduction of the liturgical renewal. Within the hierarchy national liturgical commissions were set up wherever they did not yet exist, such as in the Congo. This function was usually delegated to a bishop who then chose his collaborators from among the priests and lay people.

It must be said, first of all, that this renewal was accepted in almost every instance by both the clergy and the laity, and that it was put into practice with the utmost goodwill. Where the people had had the advantage of an immediate preparation (*e.g.,* through sermons and conferences, as in the Congo), the renewal was received with enthusiasm. It was leading them to the goal of achieving a better expression of their own religious sensibilities and expectations. In some other countries where the people suffer from the previously mentioned backwardness in liturgical matters in the mother countries, there was some hesitation, but there, too, the goodwill was obvious. Thus, during the month of October, 1965, I gave, in various places of Nigeria, with the cooperation of the State University, a number of days of liturgical formation in which all the priests were required to take part, so that the liturgical renewal could be put into practice, and ways and means for further development could be organized.

In the countries where the liturgical renewal has penetrated somewhat further, as in the Congo (Leopoldville), several regional days of study have been organized under the direction of the bishop, or the chairman of the national commission, since the reintroduction of the Liturgical Commissions. On these occasions urgent problems were discussed, such as the application of the new *Ritus servandus* (which must be looked upon rather as a starting point than as a definitive statement), the thorny question of translations in the various languages, and the problem of adaptation, both in general and in particular. Insofar as the *Ritus servandus* is concerned, various requests were formulated which the episcopal conference was asked to put before the Council, including, among other things, the translation of the principal prayers and the concluding doxology of the Canon into the vernacular.

7. In regard to the use of the vernacular, the bishops usually went as far as they possibly could. Recently, various episcopal conferences, like that of the Congo (Leopoldville), have permitted the preface to be said in the vernacular (by virtue of an indult of April 27, 1965). The reasons for using the vernacular are stronger in Africa than elsewhere. A strange and unintelligible language is regarded here as some element of magic; therefore, the use of Latin strengthens that sense of magic and is an obstacle to the formation of a genuine sense of Christian worship.

This is why the question of the translation of the *liturgical texts* is of the utmost importance. However, it is not an easy problem to solve. Most of our African peoples still live in a culture that is mainly "oral". This has tremendous advantages in that the spoken word still has its full original force (when a father curses his son, the son will die). But it has also great disadvantages, such as the vast number of languages and dialects. There has not yet been time enough for a common language to impose itself and overcome national particularism. A happy exception is the Swahili-speaking group of Tanzania, Kenya and the western part of the Congo (Leopoldville). In some other countries, French was simply introduced as the liturgical language, which was an understandable emergency solution. Elsewhere the principal African languages were used for the liturgy (cf. *Notitiae*[3] 1, pp. 55ff.), but there are too many of these for the sound application of a vernacular liturgy. While all rejoiced at the recognition of the vernacular in the liturgy, the importance of the use of a more widely used language seems to have been forgotten. It seems absolutely vital to me that we encourage the

[3] See footnote 2, p. 84.

emergence of some languages to serve as a medium for a group of other languages.

The *translation itself* creates more difficult problems in our countries because there is no written liturgical language already in existence and the work has to be done by a handful of people who are already overburdened. Therefore, it may be useful to see how they are handling the problem at Leopoldville:

(a) Psalms, hymns, the prayers and readings are translated by a special subcommission for each, at which a qualified expert is always present.

(b) The work done by these subcommissions is brought together and checked (particularly for the langauge) by a central commission.

(c) Everything is then thoroughly checked by the liturgical commission, in which the experts take part, and which is presided over by the bishop and whoever is in charge of the central commission for the whole lingual territory.

(d) Finally, the texts are sent out to the dioceses and parishes where practical use will show whatever corrections are still required. This work demands a very great effort because of the linguistic territory involved, but the results are rewarding.

8. Insofar as the publication of liturgical books is concerned, there were usually already in existence abbreviated rituals and translations of the books of the New Testament, or at least of the four gospels, although we have to admit to our shame that in the past we have devoted greater efforts to the translation of the catechism than to that of the Word of God. As to the prayers, the style and *cursus* of the Roman missal prayers are so different from the African style that here something new must be created, even if we use the themes of the Roman prayers. Insofar as the sung pieces are concerned, it is obvious that here, too, we cannot do anything with those long texts of the *Introit,* etc.: we shall have to lift the most relevant text out of these pieces and use it as a chorus to be inserted between the verses of the psalm, in the manner already suggested in the *Graduale Simplex.*

For the present, most African countries have been granted an indult to use the paraphrases of former days for the Ordinary of the Mass and suitable hymns for the Proper of the Mass. This is a very good temporary solution. In Leopoldville, therefore, a song book has already been published for the faithful, the *Toyembani Misa,* which provides suitable selections for all Sundays and feast days throughout the year, with good African music and usually of sound liturgical inspiration. However, it would appear that few linguistic regions are already that far advanced.

9. Yet, ultimately, much more than translation is involved. Translation is but the first step toward *an indigenous African liturgy which is the expression of what lives in the depths of the African soul,* and which differs in many respects from what moves the people of the West, even where the renewed liturgy of the West is concerned. We are fully aware of the fact that all of our bishops, native clergy and missionaries have been reared in the Roman liturgy, and so we shall have to start from there. But we have no right to tie our people with their need for warmth and color, dramatic expression, movement and a sense of community, to a ritual expression that is so completely at variance with African sensibility. If we do this, our people will be sorely repressed in their religious spontaneity and they will likely turn to some kind of voodoo cult, leaving the "official" liturgy to the clergy, just as Negroes have done all over the world whenever their religious feelings were not respected, and this in spite of all the talk about the rise of a "universal civilization".

We also realize that all this is a long-term and delicate operation. But we must keep our eye on the goal right from the start. The work must be done scientifically, as it is being done in our liturgical course at Lovanium University in Leopoldville. We shall also need "text centers" where people, set free from other duties, devote themselves wholly to liturgical worship and monastic foundations, such as that of Leopoldville and others. If ever the African, with his deep religious sense, is given the chance to make his contribution to the Church's worship, the whole People of God will be enriched and blessed (my own writings on this subject are spread over too far a field to be referred to here).

Enrique Rau/*Mar del Plata, Argentina*

Liturgical Reform in Latin America

Latin America as a Whole

The Constitution on the Sacred Liturgy as applied to Latin America is better studied, I think, in terms of the problems it posed than of particular events, dates and personalities. Generally speaking, its reforms were well received. The laity accepted them with interest and in some cases with real enthusiasm. Among religious, nuns seem to have paid more attention to them than priests. Our "separated brethren" have welcomed them, particularly for the new emphasis they place on the ministry of the *Word*. Non-Christians have regarded liturgical reforms with sympathy as one more sign of the efforts at renewal and adaptation being made by the Church during the Council. One of the best results achieved has undoubtedly been that through active participation in the liturgy we have acquired a deeper feeling for the "Church", the "community".

There is, however, still an urgent need for deeper knowledge of the content of the reforms: there can be no reform without previous instruction or catechesis. The pastoral lessons of the liturgy must also be integrated in the overall pastoral mission. In this way our people will be saved from the religious ignorance they presently experience.

After the promulgation of the Constitution, CELAM (The Council of Latin American Bishops) set up a Liturgical Department, organized on a continent-wide basis. Tremendous efforts have been made. Enthusiasm for the liturgical reforms is spreading throughout the continent: there are courses, publications, institutes, visits, etc. But this Department cannot yet be expected to exercise much influence on the Episcopal Conferences. It may be better for the reform to work from below upward so that it take root first in each country, and, within each country, in each diocese and parish—always, of course, in conformity with the conciliar decrees. A uniform solution imposed from above runs the risk of falling into mere formalism. Here it might be noted that the *clergy* have not yet taken sufficient notice of the importance of the *Word*.

Translation of the liturgical texts is a problem throughout Latin America, and one that raises a number of difficulties. For some, the solution is a common translation for the whole of Latin America and even for the whole Spanish-speaking world. Others would prefer to see diversity in unity, with each country finding its own solution. To understand how serious this problem is, one must remember that although all Latin-American countries (except Brazil) speak Spanish, there are considerable linguistic differences between some areas and others. Experience constantly shows that the people take part with greater care and enthusiasm in the prayers and chants of the liturgy when these are in the language they use every day, but maintaining the dignity proper to worship. Surely the Church, having broken away from the Latin language, which the people did not understand, cannot now impose turns of phrase, vocabulary and speech patterns that are alien to the people. Now that the new *Lectionaries* are widely used, one constantly hears the exclamation: "Now we understand the Gospel." This problem is, I believe, more serious than some schools of thought consider it to be.

This solution would of course raise difficulties in those countries that do not yet have their own text; however, this problem is not insuperable. CELAM has begun publishing the main liturgical texts. The Episcopal Liturgical Commission in Argentina has published a translation of the principal texts of the Mass; the translation of the remainder is almost finished and work has begun on the Ritual. Since numerous translations existed before the promulgation of the Constitution, room for choice exists. The Episcopal Conferences have either decided, or are in a position to decide, which translation is best fitted to the genius of each country. This must in any case be the first step, even if a greater degree of uniformity is later to be sought for all Spanish-speaking countries, based on the experiences gained in each country or region.

Progress must be organic, springing from the basic reality of our people, since the text is for them. The process must be gradual, and each stage may take a long time. This is the only way.

There have been various Latin American "Dialogues", including some with other Churches, to try to find, for example, a common wording for the *Our Father,* the *Creed,* the dialogue with the celebrant, etc. These efforts still have to be implemented.

Argentina

The most important factor in channeling reform along the lines laid down by the Constitution has certainly been the "Liturgical and Pastoral Directorate of the Argentinian Hierarchy", with its *Annex,* published after the appearance of the *Instructio.* This is the *official* guide.

Thanks to the *unity* with which the Argentinian hierarchy approached this vital task of renovating the liturgy, the "Episcopal Liturgical Commission", composed of five bishops, five advisors with a consultative vote and seventeen associate advisors, has been able to publish the most essential liturgical books for the whole country. Two *Lectionaries* (Epistles and Gospels); *Let Us Go to Mass:* a missal for Sundays and feast days; *Holy Father:* the Ordinary of the Mass; *Glory to the Lord:* an anthology of hymns; *Forty-two Psalms,* with words and music; several "Services of the Word" for places where there are hardly any priests, etc. It has also organized several "Liturgical Meetings" with the Diocesan Liturgical Conferences which now exist in practically every diocese. At the most recent one there were about a hundred priests and the theme was the *Homily.*

There are two problems to be faced in the near future: the restoration of places of worship (renovation of altars, images, whole churches), and, secondly, the difficult problem of *music* for the Spanish texts already approved. A special Artistic sub-commission has been established to deal with the first problem. There are two schools of thought on the musical question: one would like completely new forms; the other would rather adopt Gregorian Chant to the Spanish texts. The first school is prevailing at the present time, at least in the Commission itself. A great Competition for Liturgical Chant is being prepared, and all Spanish-speaking musicians will be asked to take part.

In conclusion, one can say that reform is under way throughout Latin America. Within the course of this year we hope to achieve a coordination of all the efforts that are being made so as to reach a unity within the beautiful and admirable variety of this continent. We are all, as young nations, eager to progress, gradually but firmly, along the ways opened up at the Council.

Godfrey Diekmann, O.S.B./*Collegeville, Minn.*

Liturgical Practice in the United States and Canada

No comprehensive survey has as yet been undertaken in either the United States or Canada to discover the state of liturgical practice before and after the promulgation of the Constitution on the Sacred Liturgy. However, sufficient data is available to permit a reasonably accurate estimate.

In the United States, it was only in 1958 that the National Conference of Bishops decided to establish an official Bishops' Commission on the Liturgical Apostolate. By that time, the liturgical movement itself had a grass-roots history of more than a quarter century. In 1926 Father Virgil Michel, O.S.B., launched the monthly magazine *Orate Fratres* (now *Worship*) and established the Liturgical Press at St. John's Abbey, Collegeville, Minnesota. Significant for the pastoral orientation of the movement from its very outset was his close friendship with Dom Lambert Beauduin, as well as his personal expert interest in social action. In his numerous writings and lectures, the liturgy was never isolated to the sanctuary; Christian living was viewed as a whole, with the liturgy as its spiritual dynamo. He therefore warmly supported two friends, Tom and Dorothy Coddington, who in the early thirties began publication of a periodical entitled *Liturgy and Sociology*—surely a unique prophetic phenomenon in the story of the modern liturgical renewal. After

157

Father Virgil's death in 1938, the sociological dimension continued to be stressed preeminently by Father H. A. Reinhold, who for the next fifteen years contributed a monthly column, "Timely Tract", to *Orate Fratres*.

The pastoral purpose of the movement was brought most effectively to nationwide consciousness by the Liturgical Weeks held annually since 1940. It was chiefly to sponsor these meetings that the National Liturgical Conference came into being. Though increasingly encouraged by individual members of the hierarchy, several of whom served terms as its president, the Conference has retained its unofficial status. Its officers and board of directors, comprising clergy, religious and laity, have within the past decade been especially representative of the country's outstanding liturgical scholars as well as pastoral leaders. In 1955, the National Liturgical Weeks were renamed the North American Liturgical Weeks, in order to indicate the growing collaboration with neighboring Canada. The Conference's activities have, moreover, been vastly expanded in recent years, so that presently its busy Washington headquarters are, practically speaking, the spearhead of our pastoral-liturgical movement, with a many-faceted publicational, educative and promotional program.

The official Bishops' Commission on the Liturgical Apostolate, formed in 1958, was instrumental in encouraging the establishment of diocesan liturgical commissions in accordance with the 1958 Instruction. In too many instances, unfortunately, the nominations to these commissions were largely honorific (monsignorial titles are no guarantee of liturgical interest or competence). The spirit to infuse life into the dry bones was thereby delayed several years. The Bishops' Commission also deserves credit for the distribution of the new version of the *Collectio Rituum* in 1961, although the actual preparation of that edition was the work of an *ad hoc* committee appointed by the bishops. It was intended, moreover, to serve as a liaison between the hierarchy and the Liturgical Conference; its secretary reported on the Conference's work and on the general state of the liturgical renewal each year at the time of the Bishops' annual meetings. In Canada, although there is a single National Bishops' Conference, distinct Bishops' Commissions on the Liturgical Apostolate have been appointed for the English and French language areas of the country, with a secretariat common to both.

Joseph Cardinal Ritter of St. Louis, Archbishop Paul Hallinan of Atlanta, and Bishop Albert Martin of Nicollet, Canada, served as members of the conciliar Liturgy Commissions during the first and second sessions of the Council. Their regular and detailed reports to their respective bishops' meetings on the Commission's mind and work no doubt contributed decisively to the vigorous support the latter received from these two hierarchies. In 1963, Archbishop Hallinan was made a member of the American Bishops' Commission on the Liturgical Apostolate, and subsequently became its secretary, while Bishop Martin has been appointed his French-Canadian counterpart.

Following the promulgation of the Constitution on the Sacred Liturgy, the American Bishops' Commission undertook to select translations of the liturgical texts, submitting them in early 1964 to the body of bishops for approbation. At a plenary meeting of the bishops on April 2, 1964, the use and extent of the vernacular were decided, and its decrees were confirmed by the Liturgical Consilium on May 1. Since there was already in existence a plan to prepare a translation of liturgical texts for use throughout the English-speaking world, the translations approved by the American bishops were taken from those already in existence. English-speaking Canada has for the most part adopted the same texts as the U.S., whereas the French-speaking dioceses have taken advantage of the publications of France.

Of all the liturgical reforms initiated by the Council, the extended use of the vernacular was beyond compare the most ardently awaited. In the United States, it was effectuated in three stages: the vernacular divine office was immediately allowed in May, 1964, because a suitable translation was already at hand; a new vernacular *Collectio Rituum* was introduced on September 14; November 29, the first Sunday of Advent, was set as the date for the vernacular in the Mass, for by then the new Missal would be ready. The reason for the different dates was solely that of availability of printed texts. Nevertheless, a current of resentment became noticeable among the laity because of the seeming favoritism shown the clergy, particularly when, as happened occasionally, some of the clergy eagerly adopted the vernacular breviary while showing little enthusiasm for the prospect of the vernacular in Mass.

To meet the widespread impatience, several dioceses officially (and a scattering of priests arbitrarily) anticipated the announced November date. A similar and certainly more vocal impatience made itself felt almost immediately after the vernacular was generally introduced, for the Collects, the embolism of the Our Father (not to speak of the Preface), as well as the dialogue preceding any Latin text, had remained in Latin. The resulting linguistic mish-mash satisfied no one. There ensued a lively "black-market" buying of the new Missal for English-speaking Canada, where most of these elements were allowed in the vernacular. While we can now look forward confidently to having all these texts in English by early 1966, a fateful precedent may have taken root in some circles whereby, in reaction to an exaggerated legalistic observance of the past, arbitrary solutions are sought to obviously unreasonable and less meaningful rubrics. For the popular liturgical watchword today is "sincerity of sign". The problem in the United States, therefore, is perhaps not so much unwillingness on the part of some to accept reforms already decreed, as an impatience on the part of a growing minority with what they consider the slow pace of the heralded thoroughgoing changes.

Insofar as the vernacular breviary is concerned, episcopal authorizations in almost all dioceses were generous, and within the year an overwhelming majority of priests were praying in English. Those who could not, such as religious bound to choral office, were agitating for permission.

The next major landmark of liturgical reform was March 7, 1965, the date for application of the Instruction of the previous September. To meet this challenge more effectively, as well as to better direct the entire national liturgical renewal, the Bishops'

Commission announced in December, 1964, the establishment of a permanent secretariat in Washington, appointing as its first secretary Father Frederick McManus. This choice met with general deep approval, for Father McManus had long been closely identified with the liturgical movement in the United States (he was currently serving his fourth term as president of the National Liturgical Conference), and was likewise a consultor of the conciliar Liturgy Commission. Presently he is a consultor of the post-conciliar Consilium. The Washington secretariat is to coordinate the work of the Bishops' Commission and to prepare materials for submission to the national body of bishops. One of its first steps was the appointment of a Music Advisory Board to make proposals for musical settings of the liturgical chants of celebrant and ministers.

Writing in the May, 1965, issue of *Notitiae,* Cardinal Ritter reported: "It would seem accurate to say that no significant difficulties were encountered on these first steps in liturgical renewal within the United States. Where, in individual instances, difficulties were encountered, they could almost invariably be traced to a lack of preparation and understanding. . . . Our people have received the liturgical renewal with enthusiasm and look forward to continued liturgical evolution with optimism." Nothing has since occurred to alter that estimate. True, considerable national publicity was for a time given to the Rev. Gommar De Pauw, who headed a "Catholic Traditionalist Movement". He claimed to speak for sixty percent of Catholics in the United States and to have the support of thirty bishops (unnamed), as well as of highly placed (unnamed) Vatican officials. As a matter of fact, every survey that has thus far been made public, whether on parochial, diocesan or wider scale, has without exception shown a strong majority, sometimes reaching above 80%, in favor of the principal changes. Most popular, predictably, was the vernacular, while the commentator, particularly in the method of exercising his role, came in for sharpest criticism. Yet, it seems a pity that the conservative view has not had a better spokesman than Father De Pauw. His extravagant charges that "liturgical changes were . . . subtly extorted from our bishops by a small but well-organized minority of self-appointed so-called liturgical experts, isolated in their ivory towers", and that "liturgical progressivism is increasingly and alarmingly appearing to many as only the first phase of a broader scheme intent to 'protestantize' the entire Catholic Church", have cast discredit on what might have proved a beneficial organization, forthrightly and competently reminding liturgists of difficulties and dangers.

Among the chief steps taken to meet "the lack of preparation and understanding" of which Cardinal Ritter wrote, the following are perhaps most significant:

1. *The Work of the National Liturgical Conference*

Excellent press coverage of the Council's discussions on the liturgy stimulated such interest that the 1963 Liturgical Week held in Philadelphia attracted 15,000 participants, and that of 1964 in St. Louis nearly 20,000, including in each case several thousand priests from all parts of the United States and Canada. In 1965, an even larger audience was reached by holding the Week in three cities: in the East (Baltimore), the Midwest (Chicago), and the Far West (Portland). Early in 1965, the Conference sponsored a study week for members of diocesan liturgical commissions, attended by over 400, and another in April for church architects and diocesan commissions on art and architecture, at which almost an equal number were present. Other such study meetings, including one for musicians, are in the planning stage. The Conference has also published a series of books and pamphlets, called "The Parish Worship Program", designed to help introduce the recent reforms, is presently sponsoring a sociological study of reactions to liturgical participation, etc.

2. *The Superb Instruction Issued by the Bishops'*
Commission to Accompany the Vernacular
Changes in the Mass

The Commission underscored the dignity and power of the spoken liturgical word, and the necessity of its proper proclamation. It spoke of the urgency of increased personal familiarity with the Scriptures, recommended parish Bible services, and reminded priests in forceful terms of their responsibilities as ministers of the Word. "By his voice, attitude, and physical bearing, the reader should convey the dignity and sacredness of the occasion. His role is that of a herald of the Word of God, his function to provide a meaningful encounter with that living Word." The document contributed substantially to counteract the very real danger of transferring slovenly habits of Latin recitation to vernacular public prayer and reading. In Canada, the Bishops' Commission has organized two national meetings of diocesan commissions, is issuing an instructive Bulletin, and sponsored a national Liturgical Week for priests, religious and laity last September.

3. National Study Weeks for the Clergy

The multiplication of such institutes is undoubtedly one of the most encouraging phenomena of the past three years in the United States and Canada. The summer of 1965 witnessed nearly twenty—theological, liturgical, biblical, pastoral, catechetical—easily averaging a hundred priests at each. The majority dealt with Scripture, but the synthesis happily occurring today in theological disciplines guaranteed that the liturgical dimension was especially prominent here, and it was absent in none. American bishops and priests can be depended on to obediently carry out the reform decrees. But only theological convictions and deepened insight into God's plan of salvation, realized in biblical history and liturgical mystery, can hope to transform the external changes into a profound and lasting spiritual renewal. We have been badly served by most of our clergy magazines in the recent past: conservative editorial policies protected readers from a knowledgeable sympthy for contemporary theological and biblical trends. The enthusiastic response on the part of older as well as younger priests to these study institutes spells a new hope. That hope becomes even brighter when we recall some concomitant developments: the two graduate institutes of liturgy

(Notre Dame University in Indiana, St. John's University at Collegeville), the sudden explosion of graduate schools in theology for religious and laity, all of which try to give due emphasis to the liturgy and the promising new catechetical movement.

4. *The Efforts of Diocesan Liturgical Commissions*

These of course vary widely, from token to total. Representative of the best is the Chicago program which enjoyed the warm support of the late Cardinal Meyer. A "Pastoral Directory on the Mass" of first-rate quality and comprehensiveness was ready by February, 1965. The 460 parishes of the diocese (the largest in the United States) were divided into fifty liturgy districts, with a "pilot parish" in each. A six-week study program prepared all priests of the diocese for the March date of the new liturgy, and a continuing program of education included the monthly mailing of a helpful recent book or pamphlet to each priest. Religious sisters were instructed through sixteen lecture hours, while an initial six-week training program for commentators, lectors and leaders of song involved no less than 11,400 laymen. The Cardinal neatly solved the divisive problem of altar-facing-people by turning the tables on those who were citing the *admiratio* argument. He wrote to his priests: "I exhort you to celebrate facing the people, so that uniformity may be had throughout the archdiocese and the people will not be exposed to '*admiratio*' by those who do not comply with the exhortations from Rome." Archbishop Cody, successor to the Chicago See, helped the cause in one of his first statements by granting permission for evening Mass every Sunday between 4 and 8 P.M. Another outstanding achievement in this category is the pastoral directory *La Construction des Eglises* issued in April, 1965, by Cardinal Léger and the other bishops of the Montreal province.

In the interests of charity, I prefer not to cite documents from the opposite end of the spectrum. But it would be fair to say that only about four or five dioceses carry on largely as if the Council hadn't happened, and that there are another few which seemingly wish it hadn't. The vast majority are honestly, even if not in every instance or in every respect knowledgeably, trying. The personal, energetic initiative (or at least firm backing) of the Ordinary proves ultimately decisive.

Of special interest is the ecumenical impact of the liturgical reforms. Symptomatic has been the attendance of several hundred Protestant ministers at each of the Liturgical Weeks since 1963 and, within the same period of time, the gain of more than a thousand new subscribers to *Worship* from the ranks of Protestant and Orthodox clergy.

What the future will hold is of course conditioned to some extent by the baggage we bring along from the present. The accelerating process of urbanization will serve only to heighten what is probably our greatest pastoral-liturgical problem: the huge city or suburban parish, militating against any experience of meaningful community. One effort, at amelioration if not at solution, is the experiment currently being made in some five dioceses of having weekday Masses in various homes, to which neighbors are invited. In any event, the role of the parish and the relevance of the traditional territorial parish are subjects of lively debate. Another factor that, paradoxically, in the minds of some priests militates against liturgical renewal is the remarkably high level of Sunday observance and of reception of the sacraments. Why criticize or tamper with what is so obviously "successful"? Only a continued and systematic theological reorientation embodying the Constitution on the Sacred Liturgy's stress on sacraments as signs of faith can bring about an understanding that this "heresy of members" might be no more than a subtle variant of the "heresy of good works".

Among expectations of future reforms, the vernacular still occupies first place. Religious obliged to choral recitation of the divine office desire it not only for the sake of improving their own prayer-life; they are almost unanimously convinced that, without it, vocations to their way of life will disastrously decrease. Moreover, now that the former fetish of the silent Canon has been exorcised by concelebration, the demand for the entire eucharistic prayer to be said or chanted aloud in the vernacular at every Mass, in order that we may fittingly "proclaim the death of the Lord until he comes", can no longer be quieted. Other hopes can be summarized under the headings of meaningful sign and avoidance of duplication. Thus, there is growing impatience with the double *Confiteor* and *Domine, non sum dignus* at Mass, the multiple crosses and genuflections during the Canon, and even with such a seemingly minor item as the obligation to re-cite the proper Introit after a reasonably suitable entrance hymn has already been sung; and the unsuitability of the present texts particularly of infant baptism and of the anointing of the sick are more than ever glaringly apparent now that the vernacular is employed.

Heartily welcomed was the explicit recognition in the liturgical reforms that uniformity is not synonymous with unity. This has roused hopes that the principle of flexibility and of adaptation to specific needs might find future expression in such matters as an alternate, simpler and more biblically worded Canon; choice within established limits of more appropriate readings for chil-dren's Masses; the possibility of substituting a set period of Scripture reading for Matins; and perhaps even of allowing lay-men to assist in the distribution of communion when there are numerous communicants. Why, finally, should not the present sharply defined categories of low, sung and solemn Masses be eliminated in favor of simply the Mass, with that degree of solemnization possible and proper to any given occasion? In a word, the Constitution on the Sacred Liturgy has not only initi-ated a new era of active participation in the sacred rites, but has sparked an unprecedented concern to obtain rites which, by their simplicity, clarity and meaningfulness in terms of contemporary man as well as of biblical and historical precedent, will more surely become the summit and fount of Christian life (Art. 10).

Heinrich Rennings/*Solbad Hall, Austria*

Progress of the Liturgical Renewal in Europe

The liturgical renewal decided upon in Vatican Council II so far covers two phases in the dioceses of Europe: (1) a period of information and preparation for the first partial reforms, and (2) the introduction of, and early reaction to, these partial reforms.

Information and Preparation

After the promulgation of the Constitution on the Sacred Liturgy in December, 1963, many Council fathers expressed their gratification at the successful conclusion of the conciliar debate on the liturgy. They did this mainly in collective pastoral letters to their fellow Christians, both clerical and lay. As the implications of the conciliar document were not easily understood, even by the clergy (apart from specialists), the bishops chose some central ideas of the Constitution and explained them. For the majority of the faithful these explanations remained largely abstract theory; they did not yet change the form of the services to which people were accustomed. Catholics were, however, impressed by the unanimity of the Council fathers at the final vote on the Constitution.

Nor did this situation change noticeably when, in the spring of 1964, a number of national hierarchies applied the recommendations contained in the apostolic letter, *Sacram Liturgiam,*

167

and allowed or prescribed the vernacular in the scriptural readings of the Mass (*e.g.,* Switzerland, France, Austria, Germany, Belgium and Portugal). This use of the vernacular had already been put into practice in several countries, although with some limitations. Further innovations, based upon the apostolic letter, aroused little interest in the various communities.

The first outspoken reactions concerned the introduction of the new formula for the distribution of communion. Many of the faithful found that the response "Amen" disturbed them in their devotion; others thought that a new formula should have been devised that was better adapted to the distribution of the body of the Lord. Reports of the progress in the preparatory measures and of the way in which people reacted to the relaxed liturgy, previously too heavily dominated by rubrics, contributed to a wider awareness of the reality of the renewal.

The national and regional commissions (set up to prepare the measures required by the reform) had to cope with, among other things, the translation of liturgical texts and the new requirements of church music and architecture. At conferences and during numerous study sessions, attention focused on general explanations; there were as yet no concrete reference points for the kind and extent of the initial stages of the reform. The instruction of *Inter Oecumenici* (which fixed the first Sunday of Lent in 1965 for the introduction of a partial reform so important for the various congregations) provoked much energetic activity because there was little time left to prepare the people. The swift and unbureaucratic methods of the Consilium (Commission for the Implementation of the Constitution on the Sacred Liturgy) deserve credit here. Some of the new Mass instructions, however, had soon to be modified again; shortly before the preparatory period expired there appeared another revised *Ritus servandus* and *Ordo Missae*. The end of the first phase was marked by a rather general uncertainty as to the future.

Steps on the Way to Reform, and the Reactions

Since the reform documents emphasize that due account must be taken of the local and national conditions of the various

Churches, leaving the extent of the changes largely to the episcopal conferences, there was a varied application of all the practices now allowed. For the Mass in general, though in many places not for the sung Mass, the vernacular is now used for the *Ordinary of the Mass,* the *Proper of the Mass* and for the prayers. Celebration facing the people is allowed and makes it possible for all the congregation to experience the liturgy as an essentially communal action. In the administration of the sacraments, the use of the vernacular does not go far beyond the use of rituals in two languages. In general, one may say that the English-speaking countries show the greatest reluctance to change, while the French-speaking countries make the fullest use of what is now allowed. It seems worth mentioning that the countries with a longer tradition of liturgical reform movements provide more favorable conditions on several counts, but are burdened by the weight of older liturgical traditions in adapting to the post-conciliar renewal.

No one expected the reform to take place immediately and without difficulties. However necessary it is to aim at a more balanced judgment, the constructive and negative reactions and experience have made certain general contributions which might help to facilitate further steps in the implementation of the reform.

The short period between the official publication of the various territorial directives and their application was not enough to provide the clergy with adequate instruction, the more so as their pastoral-liturgical training clearly reveals frightening gaps. The time limit was still less adequate for the explanatory preparation of the congregations, on which the Instruction lays so much stress (n. 4). There is a lack of literature explaining in a popular manner the aims of the reform to the members of the congregation. Any priest who wished at last to implement major changes, after all the previous unimportant changes, was tempted to ask too much at once of his congregation; this occasionally caused upheaval. In places where the clergy recognized that the whole congregation acts in the liturgical assembly (cf. Constitution, Art. 26) and began the reform with dialogue and mutual consultation with the laity, there was little resistance. How to take account of the situation of any given congregation, as one of the elements of obedience in liturgical affairs, is for many pastors a problem they cannot reconcile with the ways of thinking to which they have up until now been accustomed.

Experience shows that planning by priest and congregation together is also the best protection against the greatest danger that threatens the reform, namely, allowing the replacement of an old ceremonial by a supposedly modern one. The conciliar understanding of the Church, the new or rediscovered theological views and their practical consequences, and the spiritual revival of the faithful (cf. Instruction, nn. 5-8) as the basis and aim of the changes in the communal celebration of the liturgy, must be clearly grasped and intelligibly explained. The wish to execute the entire reform as quickly as possible overlooks the fact that the liturgical changes are embedded in the whole program of Church reform envisaged by the Council and Pope Paul VI. This reform must grow as a process of, and according to, the spirit, and not merely as a ritual and institutional development. The situation is most difficult where one, perhaps aging, priest is at the head of the congregation and, in spite of enormous goodwill, cannot himself quite understand the whole conciliar program.

For liturgical texts in the vernacular, people still rely mainly on older missals, rituals, bibles, etc., that have received provisional approval. There is widespread dissatisfaction with these translations as well as with some new ones that have been too hastily published. From the point of view of language, the translations are regretfully too close to the Latin original; from the point of view of the contents, they are too impregnated with antiquated ways of thinking and speaking. Since the present texts will have to yield to definitive ones within the foreseeable future, there is understandable skepticism with regard to the expensive double-language editions of the missal with the provisional texts, which have been announced. On economic grounds alone it would be preferable to have small booklets containing only the text of the liturgical service of the moment.

The regular reading of the biblical texts in the vernacular soon brought out the need for a richer selection of passages (pericopes). An application by the German episcopal conference to the *Consilium* for the provisional use of an extended list of passages has, because of the circumstances, been referred to higher authority but has not yet been granted. The homily as a regular part of liturgical services has found less difficulty in principle than in practice.

The grave problems in church music, created by the reform of the liturgy, exist in all countries, whether or not they already had a tradition of singing in the vernacular. If not, something entirely new has to be started, and this is the more difficult because of the provisional state of the texts; if so, the customary singing does not correspond to the requirements of the liturgy, and this leads to neglect of singing, or to a meaningless substitute when there is a desire to observe the regulations carefully. Some modest attempts have been made to arrive at a solution for the conflict between Latin and vernacular singing.

The directives for the interior arrangement of the churches have pleased the architects. At long last they have been given a program to guide them in the building of new churches. In the rearrangement of existing seating accommodations, an altar closer to the congregation and a kind of ambo have been introduced in many places; more often an unsuitable arrangement leads to obstructed viewing and awkward movements. The difficulty that some people have in understanding that the tabernacle may be separated from the altar shows just how deeply ingrained a one-sided instruction in the faith can be.

A gratifying sign of lively public opinion in the Church was the number of discussions provoked by the changes. These were even echoed in letters to the editor in non-Catholic periodicals. Occasionally, too, displeasure was expressed in minor protest activities and organized meetings. The majority of the faithful, however, agrees with the need for a reform and gratefully accepts its aims in a positive manner. The discussions about the extent and speed of the process treat all the considerations that the Council fathers had already put forth at the debate during the first session. The dialogue, started at the Council, is carried on to good purpose in the communities of the faithful. It is clear once again that the number of negative reactions is in no way representative. Moreover, many reservations are directed only against too much haste or impropriety in the proceedings. Sometimes the liturgical changes are seized upon as an outlet to give vent to anxiety about the change affecting the Church as a whole. It is hardly surprising that the old threadbare arguments that, in the past, were used in official quarters to justify the state of the liturgy that is now recognized as needing reform, are today being raised against this very reform.

If from time to time the old and the new go their separate ways, this is normal for any transition period and even has its advantages. The reform is not a regular implementation of a fixed project by order of a military general staff; it develops its own force as a communal search by all members of the Church for the right way of conducting themselves on the occasions when they meet. Nothing would be more disastrous than to stop halfway because of difficulties. As B. Fischer says: "When you have walked about in a plaster cast for a long time and it is finally taken away, you know quite clearly that your natural condition has returned to normal; and yet, at first, you feel somehow uncomfortable. The liturgical reform will no doubt bring with it some of this discomfort for the faithful. But soon this will be replaced by the happy feeling that the normal and natural condition has been restored."

BIOGRAPHICAL NOTES

JOSEPH LÉCUYER, C.S.SP.: Born August 14, 1912, he joined the Holy Ghost Fathers and was ordained in 1936. After studying in Paris and at the Gregorian University in Rome, he received doctorates in both philosophy and theology. He has been a Professor at the Pontifical Institute *Regina Mundi* and at the John XXIII Institute of the Lateran University in Rome, and is now the Procurator-General of the Holy Ghost Fathers. In addition to many articles in theological journals, he has written the following books: *Abraham notre Père, Le Sacerdoce dans le Mystère du Christ, Le Sacrifice de la Nouvelle Alliance, Etudes sur la Collégialité épiscopale* and *Prêtres du Christ.*

AMBROOS-REMI VAN DE WALLE, O.P.: Born November 4, 1927, in Aalter, Belgium, he joined the Dominicans and was ordained in 1953. After his studies at the Dominican College in Louvain and the Saulchoir in Paris, he received the licentiate in theology and is presently a candidate for the doctoral degree. The Professor of Dogmatic Theology at the Dominican College in Louvain, he has published *God die mijn jeugd verblijdt* (God, who gives joy to my youth), a work since translated into French, Spanish, German and Italian.

CASIANO FLORISTÁN: Born November 4, 1926 in Arquedas, Spain, he was ordained for the diocese of Pamplona in 1956. He pursued his studies at the Pontifical University of Salamanca, at Innsbruck and at Tübingen, receiving his doctorate in theology from the University of Tübingen. At present he is Professor of Pastoral Theology and Liturgy at Salamanca and Director of the Pastoral Theology Institute there. His publications include *Al Año Liturgico,* and *La Parroquia communidad eucaristica.*

HELMUT HUCKE: Born March 12, 1927 in Kassel, Germany. He studied at the Musikhochschule and at the University of Freiburg im Breisgau, where he earned his doctorate with the thesis, "Untersuchungen zum Begriff 'Antiphon' und zur Melodie der Offiziumsantiphonen". He is Editor of the *Neuen Psalmenbuch,* co-Editor of the review *Musik und Altar,* Assistant at the Musicological Institute of the University of Frankfurt and Head of the Musical Department of the German Historical Institute in Rome. He is the author of several important articles in musicology.

✠ HUGO AUFDERBECK: Born March 23, 1909, in Hellefeld, Germany, he was ordained for the diocese of Fulda in 1936. On September 5, 1962 he was consecrated Suffragan Bishop of Erfurt. He is in charge of pastoral activities in Magdeburg, and has written the following works: *Die Feier der 40 und 50 Tage; Aedificare; Congregare;* and *Pastoral-Katechetische Hefte.*

THOMAS VISMANS, O.P.: Born January 6, 1914 in Rotterdam, Netherlands, he joined the Dominicans and was ordained in 1937. He has studied at the Angelicum, the Institute of Christian Archaeology in Rome and the Pontifical Oriental Institute in Rome, receiving his doctorate in theology from the Angelicum in 1942. He is Professor of Liturgy at the Studium Generale of the Dominicans in Nijmegen, Netherlands, and until recently was Professor of Liturgy at the Angelicum in Rome. He is the author of *Kritische Bibliographie der Liturgie* (ET:1961) and *De Plaats van de liturgie in het godsdienstig leven.*

RÉNÉ REBOUD: Born January 4, 1914, in Friville, France, he was ordained for the diocese of Amiens in 1938. He attended the Institut Catholique in Paris, the Angelicum in Rome, and the Sorbonne in Paris, and received degrees in philosophy, literature and theology. He is Secretary General of the *Association Saint-Ambroise pour le chant sacré du peuple,* and is the composer of highly-regarded liturgical music.

ERHARD QUACK: Born January 5, 1904, in Trippstadt, Germany, he is Cathedral Choir Master, Director of the Episcopal Institute of Church Music in Speyer, and the Associate Editor of *Musik und Altar.* In addition, he has composed many choral works and music for the organ.

STEPHEN MBUNGA: Born in 1927 in Lituhi-Nyasa, Tanzania, he was ordained for the diocese of Peramiho in 1957. He has studied at the Mission Institute of the Congregation *De Propaganda Fide,* at the African Institute of the University of London, and at the Institute of Music of the University of Cologne. His publications include *Misa "Baba Yetu"* and *Church Law and Bantu Music,* and some musical compositions.

✠ WILHELMUS VAN BEKKUM: Born March 13, 1910, in Achterveld, Netherlands, he joined the Society of the Divine Word, was ordained in 1935 and consecrated Bishop in 1951. He is at present Bishop of Ruteng, Indonesia.

✠ GUILFORD C. YOUNG: Born November 10, 1916, in Sandgate, Australia, he was ordained for the diocese of Hobart in 1939. On September 8, 1948, he was consecrated Bishop. He received his doctorate in theology in 1940, and has been Professor of Sacramental Theology at the Seminary in Banyo, and Secretary of the Apostolic Delegation in Sydney. Since 1955 he has been Archbishop of Hobart.

PAUL BRUNNER, S.J.: Born December 20, 1920, in Mulhouse, France, he joined the Society of Jesus and was ordained in 1953. He pursued his theological studies in Shanghai and at the University of Trier, Germany, receiving his doctorate in theology in 1960. His publications include: *A Commentator's Handbook, Our Community Mass* and *Glory to the Lord.*

BONIFATIUS LUYKX, O. PRAEM.: Born February 6, 1915, in Lommel, Belgium, he joined the Norbertine Fathers and was ordained in 1940. He received his doctorate in theology from the University of Louvain. He was a Consultor on the Preparatory Commission on the Liturgy for Vatican Council II and is presently a member of the Conciliar Commission for the Implementation of the Constitution on the Sacred Liturgy ("Consilium"). He is a regular contributor to many theological journals, among them *Worship* and *Journal of Religion,* and has written eight books, the latest of which is *Conférences sur la Messe.*

✠ ENRIQUE RAU: Born September 29, 1899, he was ordained for the diocese of Mar del Plata in 1922 and consecrated Bishop on July 1, 1951. He received his doctorate in philosophy in 1918 and his doctorate in theology in 1922. At present he presides over the National Committee on the Liturgy and is a member of the Conciliar Commission for the Implementation of the Constitution on the Sacred Liturgy ("Consilium"). In addition to his many writings, he is the founder of *Revista de Teologia* and of *Psallite* (a scholarly journal dealing with sacred music).

GODFREY DIEKMANN, O.S.B.: Born in 1908 in Roscoe, Minnesota, U.S.A., he became a Benedictine, and was ordained June 28, 1931. He studied at the Collegio di Sant' Anselmo in Rome and at the Liturgical Institute in Maria Laach, Germany, and earned his doctorate in theology with the thesis, "De imagine Dei in homine secundum Tertulliani Scripta". He is Professor of Patrology at St. John's Seminary, and Professor of Theology at St. John's University, both in Collegeville, Minnesota. His interests and activities are mainly in the liturgical field. He is Editor of *Worship,* a member of the Executive Board of the National Liturgical Conference, and a Consultor to the Post-Conciliar Liturgical Commission ("Consilium").

HEINRICH RENNINGS: Born July 9, 1926 in Moers, Germany, he was ordained for the diocese of Münster in 1955. After studying at Innsbruck and Münster, and at the Institut supérieur de Liturgie in Paris, he received a doctorate in philosophy in 1952 and a doctorate in theology in 1965. He has been an Instructor in Liturgy at Trier and has also been active in the Liturgical Institute there. He is Editor of the series *Lebendiger Gottesdienst* started in Münster in 1961.

International Publishers of CONCILIUM

ENGLISH EDITION
Paulist Press
Glen Rock, N. J., U.S.A.
Burns & Oates Ltd.
25 Ashley Place
London, S.W.1

DUTCH EDITION
Uitgeverij Paul Brand, N. V.
Hilversum, Netherlands

FRENCH EDITION
Maison Mame
Tours/Paris, France

GERMAN EDITION
Verlagsanstalt Benziger & Co., A.G.
Einsiedeln, Switzerland
Matthias Grunewald-Verlag
Mainz, W. Germany

SPANISH EDITION
Ediciones Guadarrama
Madrid, Spain

PORTUGUESE EDITION
Livraria Morais Editora, Ltda.
Lisbon, Portugal

ITALIAN EDITION
Editrice Queriniana
Brescia, Italy